Acclaim for *Leading in ~~Crisis~~*
Managing Pai...
Mis...

"The once-in-a-lifetime pai ... ...sis has made it more evident than ever before that global leadership requires a nuanced understanding of the interplay of local, national and transnational trends in a constantly changing environment. Through their deep experience, the authors of this important book articulate the principles of successful leadership in crisis, not just as ideas but as concrete plans for action."

Vishakha Desai, *Senior Advisor for Global Affairs to the President and Chair of Committee on Global Thought, Columbia University.*

"This is an extremely timely and very practical look at leadership actions in managing crises. The authors combine years of experience in crisis management in a way that can be applied not only to the current COVID-19 crisis, but to future crises. It is an unusual book for unusual times and should be read by anyone who believes that they will have to manage through crises in the uncertain world ahead."

Stephen Rhinesmith, Ph.D., *author, former special ambassador to the Soviet Union and one of the world's leading expert on global leadership.*

"I have had the good fortune to have led an international aid agency, the U.S. Agency for International Development. The mission of USAID has two aspects: long-term development and humanitarian relief. The first part relates to improving the lives of people who live in developing societies and preventing those societies from descending into deep poverty and chaos. The second provides rescue, shelter, food and medical care when disaster strikes. When prevention fails, relief from harm is the only option. Both aspects require planning and preparation, the elements that make this book so relevant. Denton and Lally have provided timely advice for any organization that wishes to thrive in a world beset by challenges that do not respect sovereign borders: infectious disease; climate-related disasters; violent conflict and forced migration. The answer is not to retreat, but to identify risk and plan for the worst while taking all the necessary preventive steps. This requires inspired and informed leadership of the kind this volume advocates. Read it and prepare!"

J. Brian Atwood, *Former Administrator, USAID*

"Hundreds of millions of people are affected by the Covid-19 pandemic. In times of crisis, one wonders how the right decisions are made and by whom. This book illustrates what it takes to get through the storm without making any big mistakes: be prepared, have the right crisis toolkit in place, and apply the right leadership skills. This book includes many practical and dramatic examples from the world of a global nonprofit, complemented by a career crisis trainer's wealth of experience. Having read this book, you will know what will work and what will not, which could be a lifesaver in the next big crisis."

Dr. Willibald Plesser, *Partner at Freshfields Bruckhaus Deringer, a leading international law firm, and Chair of the Risk Committee of a global nonprofit organization.*

"In the end, crisis plans are just words on paper. They come to life only when put into action by a crisis response team that is empathetic, ethical, principled, and ready to lead. Denton and Lally's honest and thoughtful reflection on how global organizations have responded to the COVID-19 pandemic illustrates this very principle. And, because leadership must be demonstrated at all levels of an organization, this book is an excellent primer for anyone within their organization's crisis response function."

Christopher Lukach, *APR, President, AKCG – Public Relations Counselors*

"At times, we learn our best lessons under the harshest conditions. This was never more true than it is now. Even as we have yet to emerge from the effects of the pandemic, the authors have distilled important lessons to guide us all through the tough months ahead and for years to come as we rebuild education abroad from the ground up."

Melissa Torres, President and CEO of The Forum on Education Abroad.

LEADING IN CRISIS:

Managing Pandemics and Other Misfortunes

Hal Denton and Fiona Lally

Leading in Crisis: Managing Pandemics
and Other Misfortunes

The authors previously published *No Complaints, No Lawsuits: the Eleven Guiding Principles of Quality Risk Management*, 2018

Editor: Laurie R. Denton
Cover Design: Jack Pirtle
Illustrations: Francesca Lally
Cover Photograph, 2011 by Darryl Jack

Dedication

AFS stands on the shoulders of the AFS volunteer ambulance drivers, and we were never more aware of that than in this pandemic. So we dedicate this book to these visionaries, to the AFS International crisis management team, especially Larry, David and Maria and the AFS crisis teams around the world who continue to work tirelessly to keep the AFS vision and mission alive, to the courageous participants who exemplified the AFS spirit under the most challenging circumstances, and to all AFS returnees for continuing the dream of peace through understanding.

Table of Contents

Preface

And once the storm is over, you won't remember how you made it through, how you managed to survive. You won't even be sure whether the storm is really over. But one thing is certain. When you come out of the storm, you won't be the same person who walked in. That's what this storm's all about.—**Haruki Murakami, Japanese writer**

Most of us first heard of a new coronavirus in mid-to late January 2020. It appeared serious, but at first it appeared to be confined to China. Facts were hard to come by. What none of us could have known then was that this new virus would sweep the globe like a slow-moving tsunami and would overwhelm us and change our world. This tragic pandemic has created a crisis like no other in recent history.

Other crises may have been more deadly, but at least four things make this pandemic unique:

1. This crisis has been enduring and evolving, affecting everyone around the world in ways we have not seen since the 1918 Spanish Flu pandemic.

2. Air travel has made it extremely difficult to stop rapid and extensive global transmission of a virus that can be spread by asymptomatic or pre-symptomatic people.

1

3. Everyone is connected to each other through social media and nonstop news, making it far too easy to politicize and polarize vast numbers of people's beliefs about the illness.

4. The world's economies are more interdependent than ever, so any country's economic shutdown can cause lasting global effects on supply chains and economic recovery.

These four factors helped to create a crisis of unprecedented magnitude, breadth, impact and velocity. The effect is that virtually everyone—from individual families to small local businesses, from large international organizations to governments—has been overwhelmed. This has happened as we have each tried to proceed using information that is often insufficient, incorrect, or misleading, making data-driven decisions almost impossible.

In crises like these, leadership is forged on the experience and qualities of leaders themselves. Each of the authors has spent more than 30 years managing crises and developing tools for crisis management. Our first book, *No Complaints, No Lawsuits; the Eleven Guiding Principles of Quality Risk Management,* provides an overview of how to prepare for and manage risk and crisis in your organization. *Leading in Crisis* explores how applying these principles and meeting the new demands of leaders in a crisis, even one of unimaginable proportions, can help steer you and your business through the uncharted and unpredictable waters of today's world.

Ultimately, crisis management is about leadership and communication. Effective leaders can keep an organization, a community, or a country aligned and working together toward the best possible solution. Poor leaders can only achieve chaotic, inconsistent responses. Precious resources (including time and skills) are squandered, opportunities are lost (because there are opportunities even in crises) and the possibility of success can turn to failure. In the case of a pandemic, the result can be catastrophic loss.

This book explores the tools most helpful in managing a crisis—evaluating crisis conditions, creating the right team and using a crisis toolkit to develop a plan. It also explores the leadership actions most critical in a crisis—clear thinking; a steady hand; agile yet careful planning; effective, clear, factual, regular communication; compassion and kindness; and the ability to make rapid-fire, difficult decisions with imperfect information and keep moving forward.

We also explore how to train for crisis scenarios and conduct a post-crisis evaluation, both critical because they inform preparation for the next crisis. And there *will* be another crisis.

Covid-19, the illness caused by this new coronavirus, led to a breakdown of many of the structures we rely on in our daily lives, leaving vast sectors of the world's population without work. Some governments responded inadequately from a crisis management perspective: from poor communications and wishful thinking to a lack of preparedness and erratic decision-making. Intentional misinformation sown through social media for political advantage compounded many governments' poor responses. Even those that responded remarkably well are still learning how to adjust to this new reality. As this book is being published, global containment of the Covid-19 pandemic is still far away.

LEADING IN CRISIS:

The experience of Covid-19 has left many in despair for the future, struggling with an unprecedented level of uncertainty in both our personal and professional lives. It is a crisis that continues to create enduring stress for everyone around the globe, which is why we believe it has changed what is required to be effective crisis leaders. Crisis managers have to step up in unprecedented ways. We will get through this storm, but we will also, just as certainly, be forever changed by it.

This book explores what we can learn from this crisis to become stronger leaders, better crisis managers, personally and professionally, and better prepared for the next crisis.

INTRODUCTION

By Fiona Lally

I started in crisis management 30 years ago, working on insurance and risk management for global organizations in 1991. I started my firm, Rasenna Consulting, Inc., which specializes in these areas. Risk management creates systems to reduce the possibility of loss for organizations, and insurance helps pay for losses when they occur.

Clients began asking me for crisis management consulting, too. "Isn't that part of your business?" they would ask. "Doesn't crisis management reduce risk and loss?" At first, I demurred, explaining this was a different area of expertise. But then I came to realize they had a point. So, I began to work on it.

Back then, my crisis management training had a heavy emphasis on industrial crises such as loss of real property and inventory, recalls, product shortages and operation backups. Those can be pretty critical if you're a brick-and-mortar business. But many of my clients were global nonprofits, for whom crises often had worldwide service and communication components. These weren't addressed by my crisis training.

In the years before the internet, before social media, we had to develop systems to help organizations manage different kinds of crises on a global scale. I began working in those days with my co-author Hal Denton, general counsel for my client, AFS Intercultural Programs, and creator and head of its risk management team.

We created a number of innovations in crisis management background, like a classification system to evaluate crises and a team structure to support the different crises we identified. We created roles, checklists and plans that we turned into a crisis toolkit. AFS has always been masterful at managing international crises. It built its skill by continuously using and refining these crisis tools. Over the years, I offered scenario-based training. Some seemed pretty far-fetched but were useful for creating crisis management muscle.

One training in 2006 featured a scenario about crisis response to a worldwide virus. "Pandemic," read a slide in the PowerPoint presentation, "could present the most complex crisis ever faced by AFS."

When the pandemic happened, of course, the tools and training proved essential. We outline them here for crisis managers to use. But what we have now all witnessed during the complex crisis of this pandemic is that even a great plan needs great leadership to be effective.

Hal's experience as crisis team leader for AFS during the pandemic shows what Covid-19 has demanded of crisis managers. Around the world, organizations have been going through similar crucibles, dealing with crises of greater scope and length than they ever imagined, sometime several at a time.

For many, crisis plans that were supposed to be saviors did not hold up.

In this book, we blend our tested crisis management tools with Hal's experience, detailing the hard-won conclusions he drew about what crisis leaders must do to surmount a pandemic. Only the right tools and the right leadership can manage crises of this scale. In this way, Covid-19 changed everything.

By Hal Denton

M y initiation into the world of crisis management came on my first day working at AFS Intercultural Programs. AFS began as the American Field Service, a self-funded volunteer ambulance corps, created in April 1915 by A. Piatt Andrew to care for those wounded in battle in World War I. The ambulance corps was reactivated in World War II with AFS ambulance drivers caring for wounded soldiers in North Africa, Italy, Europe, the Middle East and India-Burma. After that war, AFS was transformed into a groundbreaking international secondary school exchange, volunteer and intercultural learning organization that sought to avoid yet another world-wide conflagration by increasing intercultural understanding among diverse people around the globe. By the early 2000s, it was sending more than 10,000 young people aged 15–18 on programs from more than 70 sending countries to more than 70 hosting countries all over the world.

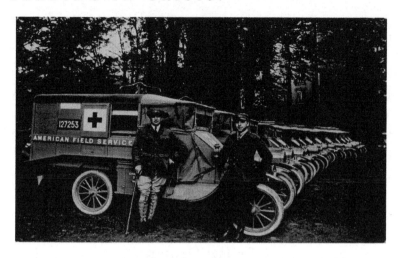

A. Piatt Andrew and Stephen Galatti shown here in WWI.
Reprinted with permission of AFS Intercultural Programs, Inc.

I had been an AFS exchange student myself, so I was excited to start work as general counsel on December 14, 1989. Within 15 minutes, I faced my first crisis. We didn't have a crisis management team back then, or even a crisis plan, but we did have experienced people who cared deeply about the AFS mission.

I had barely hung up my coat when 10 people came into my office to tell me we had just lost contact with 40 students hosted in Panama on our high school exchange program. They were in the airport on their way to a mid-stay retreat when the U.S. invaded Panama. U.S. Marines were scheduled to arrive at the airport just as our participants were preparing to leave. My colleagues asked me what I thought we should do. In a panic, I thought to myself, "How should I know? I just got here!" But we created an action plan and agreed to regroup in an hour.

Half an hour later, a large bundle arrived on my desk, a lawsuit of some sort.

I had a sinking feeling when the office manager called me up an hour after that and said, "Get up here right away!! They're trying to arrest me." I jogged up to the fifth floor to find a NY fire marshal in a heated debate with the office manager. Apparently, AFS had installed a fire alarm system that would only function in a larger building and was therefore violating city code. I was able to calm things down by agreeing to meet the next day at the marshal's office. Fortunately, soon thereafter, we received word that the participants in Panama had all been able to depart minutes before the Marines landed. All were safe and sound.

All's well that ends well, I thought. But at home as I lay awake that night, I wondered if I was up to this kind of job.

What I didn't understand then, and what has taken me years to realize, was that I was not only up to the job, I enjoyed it. It was almost as if it was my destiny to become a risk and crisis manager. In the ensuing 30 years, AFS has survived many crises. Its mission is, in part, to help 15- to 18-year-olds live with a host family they've never met, in another country, and attend school for a year. Given the nature of the mission and the dramatic changes in our world over the past 30 years, AFS has faced more than a few challenges, many rising to the level of crisis and some rising to the level of extreme crisis.

There were nights during the Covid-19 pandemic when I lay awake wondering if all of us at AFS could keep the organization going. My crisis team and I were committed to success, even though we couldn't see initially what that might look like as we closed all programs. But in September 2020, we were the first student exchange program to re-open for 500 students in 20 countries, using a traffic light system we designed to manage risks and determine where and how best to operate safely.

Fiona is a specialist in risk management and travel medical insurance and in that capacity, she helped the team deal with the numerous risk and coverage issues suddenly facing AFS at the time of the repatriations. When the questions came rolling in—would there be medical coverage for our participants now that a pandemic had been confirmed? What about testing? How about quarantine?—she had to respond rapidly and worked side-by-side with the team throughout the repatriation effort.

Throughout the book, "we" refers to the co-authors. In the sections describing the AFS experience, "we" refers to AFS or to me and the international crisis management team (the crisis team) and "I" refers to me and my role as crisis team leader.

PART ONE. PREPARING FOR A CRISIS—The AFS Case Study

LEADING IN CRISIS:

CHAPTER 1: What Is a Crisis?

A crisis is a specific kind of event; it's not just a time when things are going haywire.

Many organizations deal with problems that can be chronic or deeply difficult to manage. While challenging, they are not necessarily crises. The business of the organization can go on as usual even when a bad problem requires resolution. A crisis requires senior management to prioritize it immediately over other business to forestall significant damage.

When a crisis occurs, it's important to identify it precisely the moment it arises and to understand the exact type of crisis you are dealing with, because that will tell you when and how best to respond.

The hallmarks of a crisis are that it:

1. Is sudden,
2. Is unexpected,
3. Must be handled immediately,

4. Requires senior management attention,
5. Can have a serious impact on the organization.

Sudden. An event appears quickly, and time is not on your side.

Unexpected. If you knew the event was coming, it could still present a challenge, but with time to prepare adequately, it might not become a crisis.

Must be handled immediately. People must drop what they are doing to pay attention to it. It can't simply be managed along with the regular day's work.

Requires senior management attention. Senior decision makers need to be personally involved; the crisis response can't be delegated.

Can have a serious impact on the organization. Even if the event itself does not seem that bad at the time, its repercussions can threaten the organization.

It's not always easy to identify a crisis, particularly when it looks like something that has been manageable before. In an excellent article by Michael Marshall on why it is so difficult for people to recognize a crisis, he states: "Crises do not come out of nowhere but are the most extreme versions of things that happen all the time."

https://www.bbc.com/future/article/20200409-why-we-find-it-difficult-to-recognise-a-crisis?ocid=ww.social.link.email

This can certainly be said of Covid-19. In recent years, the world has seen outbreaks of MERS, SARS, Ebola and H1N1 epidemics, but those were contained much more quickly and more effectively than the new Coronavirus. The potential impact of Covid-19 was not fully appreciated initially by many leaders, which means that the crisis did not receive the immediate attention it required for effective control in many countries.

Since my first day in 1989, AFS has faced crises of all shapes and sizes. AFS evacuated participants hosted in Venezuela amid civil unrest in the late '90s. We also evacuated students in Egypt during the 2010 Arab Spring, from Japan during the Fukushima Daiichi nuclear disaster of 2012, and China and other countries during the SARS pandemic of 2003 and H1N1 pandemic of 2009. Because AFS sends high school students on its programs, the challenges and responsibilities differ significantly from college study-abroad programs, many of which are dorm-based and most all of which involve young adults who can legally make their own decisions.

Over the years since I first hung up my coat on that brisk December morning, my team developed a robust risk and crisis management program. We were tested in each of the cases listed above and in many others. After each crisis, we evaluated and worked hard to improve and refine our action plan. Yet nothing truly prepared us for Covid-19.

In January 2020, AFS had more than 7,000 young people living with host families far from home in school-based programs. Things were running smoothly until AFS started hearing inklings of a new virus in Wuhan, China. Information was sketchy, but AFS had no participants hosted there. Initially Wuhan was merely one of many areas of concern the crisis team was watching carefully. However, that shifted in a matter of weeks. On January 29, 2020, AFS made the difficult decision to close programs in China and Hong Kong.

The crisis team and I were concerned that the information we were receiving from Chinese officials was not reliable, and we struggled with how to make decisions with insufficient and possibly inaccurate information. For AFS, the safety of AFS stakeholders, such as participants, volunteers and staff is paramount. And participants, as the most vulnerable, are the top safety priority for AFS.

The team was deeply concerned about the risk of being unable to evacuate participants if the deadly virus spread in China. Cutting short a great experience is not something any organization wants to do, but once British Airways announced it was ceasing all service in and out of China on January 29, 2020, the team knew other airlines would soon follow. The window of opportunity to repatriate our students would likely close rapidly. This is when the crisis team assessed the potential impact of the epidemic in China on AFS.

The next 10 days were chaotic. AFS evacuated more than 200 participants in very challenging circumstances. Local AFS volunteers typically travel with AFS's teenage participants to the departure city, but this time they could not because of internal travel restrictions. Therefore, AFS grouped participants where possible and arranged for volunteers to meet them at the transfer points in their journey.

Airlines began cutting service dramatically, leaving some students with long and complex return travel. AFS booked many students on international flights that were cancelled minutes after the students arrived at the airport. That increased the stress on students, staff, volunteers, sending parents, and host families.

Managing communications was a challenge, primarily because AFS has stakeholders all over the world, across all time zones, who speak different languages and needed information on a regular basis to track each participant's situation. The AFS community includes staff and volunteers in more than 50 countries, as well as host families, schools, sending parents, and, of course, participants. Dozens, and sometimes hundreds of communications across almost every time zone were required to arrange for the successful repatriation of each participant.

Who are stakeholders?

Stakeholders are people or entities with an important interest in your operation. Most organizations have more stakeholders than they realize. This wheel shows a sample range of stakeholders for different kinds of organizations:

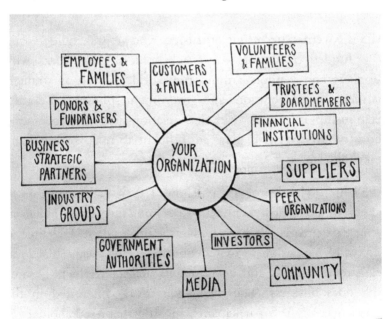

In many for-profit businesses, the emphasis is often squarely on stockholders who have a financial interest in the way the organization is managed, and customers who buy their products or services. For AFS, the customers are primarily the participants, but they are only part of a wide global network of people who share the AFS mission of intercultural understanding.

Participants come from a sending family in their home country and stay with a host family in their host country. They are supported by AFS staff in both sending and hosting countries, as well as an army of volunteers, making AFS one of the largest volunteer organizations in the world. In crises that involve emergency response or involvement by staff and volunteers, such as the evacuation effort, the families of each of the volunteers are stakeholders, too.

AFS is governed by volunteer trustees who are stakeholders, and it is funded by donors—also stakeholders. AFS works with suppliers and vendors around the world, as well as strategic partners like corporations and government sponsors where the relationship is central. AFS has relationships with peer and industry groups that play an influential role, so they are stakeholders, too.

AFS's high school program is school-based—participants go to school in their host country—so schools are stakeholders as well. Participants often need visas, and student exchange is subject to regulation in many countries. This means that local regulatory agencies and governments are stakeholders in how AFS does business. The media are always interested in the experiences of AFS participants, making them stakeholders as well. And because AFS is fully invested in cultural experiences, the communities where participants stay are also stakeholders. Community members would definitely say they are stakeholders, too.

Typically, when a crisis occurs, stakeholders want to know what's going on and often need to take action, which makes communications with stakeholders a key part of crisis management. Despite the logistical and communications challenges, the evacuation from China went remarkably smoothly, in part because evacuating participants from a country that is unsafe back to their families in countries where things are calm is something AFS has handled many times before.

LEADING IN CRISIS:

CHAPTER 2: Understanding the Type of Crisis You are Facing

The Four Levels of Crises

There are different ways to organize and evaluate the crises your organization may face. We developed an approach AFS has used for 20 years that categorizes crises in four levels, based on the extent to which each type affects stakeholder groups. To set up the right team and follow through with the right strategy, it is critical to make an immediate assessment of the level and type of crisis you're facing.

How do you gauge a crisis? Initially our impulse is often to measure its size. It's easy to visualize crises caused by big events, like an engulfing factory fire or accident, which can drive everyone's urgent response. Using that as a guide, we might figure that crises with a smaller footprint could be managed with a more modest response.

But crises can't be measured by their magnitude alone. They have to be assessed by their potential impact as the crisis unfolds. Sometimes the crises that garner the most internal attention aren't the ones that have the most profound effect. Sometimes the first steps we take to tamp down a crisis don't help mitigate its ultimate impact.

At other times, taking the correct initial steps can avert disaster. In 2014, the United States faced an Ebola outbreak, but a rapid and careful response limited its impact. Ultimately, only two people were infected on U.S. soil and neither died. Two people who had been brought to the United States for treatment passed away. This was an effective and remarkable crisis response that has been largely lost to history because it was handled so well.

Gauging a crisis correctly and responding effectively can dramatically alter its potential impact. Imagine a crisis as a bullseye. The innermost circle represents impact that is mostly internal, involving only people within your organization. Impact radiates to outer circles as more stakeholders are involved, as your reputation is threatened, as the attention of higher level of leadership is required, and a different level of coordinated response is required.

When you have a crisis plan in place and your crisis team is able to quickly assess the level of crisis—1 to 4—the team will know how to manage it from the start.

Crisis Level 1: Internal Impact—your business operations, finances, personnel or property. The big factory fire might be a Level 1 crisis for a small business if it damages the assets and threatens the continuity of the business.

A Level 1 crisis involves organizational matters but not significant injury or threat of personal safety to many people. In a Level 1 crisis, the emphasis is on managing the event within the organization. Examples of Level 1 crises are burglaries, assaults, non-fatal vehicular accidents, property damage or injury to staff or customers.

Crisis Level 2: External Impact

A Level 2 crisis typically involves an event of regional or national scope, like a hurricane, a blackout, or terrorism. Its hallmark is that you are required to deal with it even though your organization had nothing to do with causing it.

In a Level 2 crisis, it is not just your organization that is affected. Everyone else around you is, too. Sometimes the local infrastructure is damaged or gone. The difficulty in Level 2 crisis management often comes from a lack of reliable information, which diminishes options, resources and personnel.

The way you can create liability in a Level 2 crisis is by your response. Level 2 crisis management focuses on an emergency response where your primary stakeholders, such as customers, participants or employees, need swift attention but are not seriously hurt or in danger. This is why much of the strategy in a Level 2 crisis has an external focus.

Crisis Level 3: Full Impact

When an event that would otherwise be classified as a Level 1 or 2 crisis presents a significant risk of endangerment to stakeholders, we classify it as Level 3. This is because it then involves both an internal focus—dealing with the crisis—and an external focus—dealing with the negative effects of the crisis, including possible media attention. Safety and endangerment risks can present as:

1. An accident or illness simultaneously affecting several stakeholders involved in your organization's activities.

2. Significant and imminent threat to the safety of one or more people outside your organization.

A Level 3 crisis can also harm the organization because:

1. The safety and viability of the organization is threatened by the event itself, by public perception of the event or of the way your organization handles the event. A negative impact is sometimes what emerges first, causing a crisis both for the individuals involved and for the organization.

2. An individual experiencing a negative impact that arises (or he or she alleges arose) from your organization's activities.

Anything that causes harm—physical, financial, social, legal or psychological—can hurt your organization. And it can have a broad scope. Someone can allege harm from your organization's activities, even though the harm that occurred is not immediately clear.

An example is an allegation of unfair discrimination or misconduct that occurred years ago. This can create a crisis for your organization, regardless of whether you think the claim is justified. How your organization handles this or any other allegations of harm related to its activities can have a dramatic effect on your ability to carry on.

It's the interplay of interests in protecting everyone from harm—both within your organization and outside—that marks a Full Impact crisis.

Level 3 crises can manifest in many ways. They represent the broadest potential range of crises that happen at one location. Examples of Level 3 crises are: allegations of sexual misconduct, serious injury or death of a stakeholder in your care, a transportation accident involving multiple stakeholders, or civil unrest requiring evacuation of personnel.

For AFS, the risk management team determined the evacuation of participants from China was a Level 3 crisis and managed it that way. It required the full attention of the crisis team at AFS International and select staff around the world but did not require the involvement of every AFS member organization or the entire senior management team at AFS international headquarters (AFS International).

Crisis Level 4: Global Full Impact

It takes the full resources of a crisis management team to deal with a Level 3 crisis. However, sometimes a Full Impact crisis can arise in many different regions or around the world from the same event.

An example is a plane crash during an international flight. It will have a terrible global impact—for passengers and crew and their relatives around the world. This will be particularly felt in the country where the flight originated, the country where it was bound, and the place where the crash occurred, all at the same time.

A Global Full Impact Crisis can also arise from a single event that affects people in different places in the same way. A tsunami traveling continuously across oceans is an example of this kind of risk, as is a pandemic.

To manage a Level 4 crisis, organizations require full internally and externally focused teams that can mirror each other and operate simultaneously in different locations. It's important to make the Level 4 evaluation as soon as such a crisis happens, so that teams can be set up correctly right away. If that doesn't happen, it's very hard to get on top of management requirements. The need to make urgent decisions while lacking sufficient reliable data is another hallmark of Level 4 crises.

Unfortunately for AFS, as the Level 3 crisis of repatriation from China began to wind down, Covid-19 began to appear in other countries, including the United States. Covid-19 spread relatively slowly in early February, but by late February had become a massive problem. The severity of the outbreak in northern Italy caught many off guard, and soon became quite alarming.

On February 29, AFS International shared with more than 55 member organizations around the world the 12 decision-making criteria the crisis team and I developed to determine whether programs in additional countries should be closed in light of the ongoing spread of Covid-19. The team developed these at a time of extreme uncertainty about how the new coronavirus pandemic might evolve and spread, and well before the WHO declared the new coronavirus to be a pandemic.

The decision-making criteria evaluated factors such as government agency information, local health care systems, airline access, relative risk at alternate locations, quarantine possibilities and prospects for schools and host families. Italy's health care system is often rated among the best in the world, but it at that time was quickly overwhelmed by Covid-19 cases. This was a critical factor for AFS. On March 5, the Italian government announced schools would close. Because AFS is a school-based program, this was also a critical factor in assessing whether the program could continue.

One of the biggest challenges at that time was the high level of uncertainty and lack of solid information to support decision-making. Since then, it has become clear that schools can adapt by offering online learning, among other things. We also know now that physical distancing, masks, and avoiding large gatherings can dramatically slow the spread of the virus, and that governments, communities and families around the world can adapt to this new reality. But in late February and early March, the high degree of uncertainty amplified the potential risks and complicated decision-making.

AFS carefully considered the program closure criteria. In close discussion with our AFS office in Italy, and keeping participants' wellbeing at the forefront, it was clear by March 9, 2020, that the hosting program in Italy would need to close. Airlines were cutting service; schools were shut; and the team was concerned that participants with simple, common problems like appendicitis might not have access to necessary care, putting them at risk. With nearly 500 participants spread all over Italy, AFS launched another intense evacuation.

LEADING IN CRISIS:

CHAPTER 3: Creating the Crisis Team

Building Your Team

T he kind of crisis identified—Internal, External, Full Impact or Global Full Impact—determines your response. Senior management must make this determination as soon as it's clear there is a crisis. As is always the case with risk management, if the crisis is not initially diagnosed correctly, the response will not work well.

The next action after assessment is to staff the right crisis team using a combination of team members dictated by the crisis type. Crises can't be effectively managed by one person alone. They can escalate too fast and require too many actions and decisions at once. Their management requires a ready team whose members can jump into responsibilities already familiar to them.

When the crisis team leader activates the crisis team, he or she should be able to rely on all team members to deliver specific crisis-related services for which they have been trained.

The **Crisis Team Leader** should be the person most equipped to manage the crisis. This should be a senior manager, but it's often best that this person not be the head of the organization. Your company head may need to be involved in other aspects of the crisis, such as traveling to the location involved, managing media communications, or focusing on saving the organization itself in the long run. We examine the crisis team leader's job more fully in chapter 5.

Crises that have a largely internal focus will emphasize the role of the **Internal Team Member,** whose job is to focus on getting information and generating communication within the organization. An example of an internally focused crisis might involve an allegation of wrongdoing, such as by the CEO. The internal team member works on establishing the facts of what occurred and on keeping people in the organization informed.

The internal team member recruits colleagues for assistance and advises on next steps. This team member updates the rest of the team and affected stakeholders so everyone involved is working with the most current information.

Managing internal communication is sensitive work. Successful crisis teams recognize that managing internal communications is different than monitoring what is happening in the world. The team benefits from both skill sets. Many crisis teams therefore include a trained **External Team Member.**

The external team member's job is to monitor what is going on outside for decision-making. During a hurricane, for example, the external team member tracks weather reports, emergency requirements, public response and traffic and evacuation activities.

The external team member gathers information from many sources, sorting out what is going on in the world and keep the team updated with information from the media, phone calls, interviews and investigation.

The external team member contacts government authorities, business associates, embassies, peer organizations, law enforcement and medical facilities. A major part of the external team member job is to continuously vet outside information to determine its reliability, particularly if it comes from the internet or seems to be conflicting or changing. A good external team member provides regularly scheduled updates to the team, whether there are changes to report.

Social media is a key concern in a crisis but typically the **Media Contact Person** not the external team member would be the one to monitor social media. (See below for more on the media contact person.)

A Global Full Impact crisis should involve both an internal and external team member, as the crisis can require sorting out internal information, generating internal and external communication, and monitoring extensive messages from outside sources. This is especially true now with rapid and vast social media comments on you or your organization.

We separate out the roles of the internal and external team members because this reduces confusion, bias and duplication. It boosts team effectiveness when everyone knows just whom to go to for information.

A Global Full Impact crisis can be further complicated by time and language differences, because it requires teams working around the world together. Internal team members can work with affiliate internal and external team members, helping ensure rapid gathering and sharing of accurate information.

The external team member plays an important role helping the media contact. All information going to the media should be channeled through a single contact. The team's media contact should set the team's media strategy, so this is a vital role. The media contact benefits from having readily available resources, such as an up-to-date media kit and media training, as well as a solid understanding of corporate details and the mission of the organization.

The **Media Contact Person** often plays a key role in level three or level four crises and can be important in crises of any level. All direct media contact should be funneled through this person, including monitoring and responding to posts in social media. It can be a challenge to determine when to respond to online posts, but it is always important to screen for and respond to inaccurate information that may gain traction on social media.

The role of the **Documenter** is to record team decisions, so that team members know what steps to pursue and how to follow up on them. The documenter role is harder than it seems. It's neither possible nor desirable to record everything that's said in the heat of crisis. The job requires quick judgment about what to record, and an understanding of what to leave out because it is unnecessary, potentially inaccurate or speculative.

This job requires swift, constant work, so it should go to someone quite skilled. It's tiring to be a documenter, but the role is essential. It's important to keep training alternates using tabletop scenarios.

You will also need to maintain a group of knowledgeable specialty team members who can be available for quick or extended consultation on matters you anticipate could come up.

Try to make it possible for a legal contact to be on the crisis team right from the start, not just peripherally when legal issues start to appear. The legal contact can establish the type of legal advice needed, determine what other legal advisors or research may be needed, vet outgoing statements, ensure timely notification of parties such as insurers, and review decisions recorded by the documenter before they are released.

Three other specialty crisis team members often prove valuable. One is an information technology, or communications tech team member who can help maintain communications during a computer hardware or software breakdown, for example. A personnel team member can be vital in employee-driven issues. An industry or brand specialty team member can add key detail in crises that closely involve your product or social media, for example. What kind of trained specialty team members might your organization need to manage the kinds of crises that can happen to your organization? Who could you recruit and train now to assist the crisis team?

Once the team members have been assembled, the crisis team leader convenes the team as needed for meetings and conference calls. He or she helps the team keep working to inform and identify issues and manage the crisis. The crisis team leader ensures that backup team members are briefed and ready to step in when needed. He or she leads the team to de-escalate the crisis and resume normal business activities.

Leadership Role in Team-building

Build your team members before a crisis occurs, because it is much more difficult for people to both learn new roles and implement them during a crisis. This is where tabletop exercises and other forms of training can help. This is addressed more fully in chapter 15.

At the very least, it is important to have a core group who knows its roles and can move quickly. This will help ensure an environment of quiet confidence as the team moves to gain control of the crisis without alarming or panicking people unnecessarily. See chapter 12 for more on the actions you can take during a crisis to make sure your team functions at high proficiency.

Train team members in their responsibilities individually and collectively. Assign backups for each team member so that every role can be filled when needed, whether someone is on vacation or out sick. This became extremely important for AFS, as three of the key crisis team members developed Covid-19 within the first week of the global repatriation effort.

Individual crisis team roles don't change when the crisis level changes, but the team structure and size and member responsibilities do. This way your core team members and their backups can be ready to manage any kind of crisis that comes their way.

AFS viewed the evacuation from Italy as a Level 3 Full Impact crisis and staffed its crisis team accordingly, with the AFS director of risk and crisis management acting as crisis team leader. Both an internal and external member joined the team. The internal team member kept the team informed about what was happening within the organization and kept contact with the AFS organization in Italy. The external team member kept on top of developing and conflicting news about country and government decisions, the progress of the virus, airline activities, and updates for families and other stakeholders.

Unfortunately, this evacuation was only the tip of the iceberg. As AFS successfully returned participants from Italy and Italy itself struggled to manage Covid-19 outbreaks, Covid-19 cases began appearing and sometimes growing rapidly in many other parts of the world.

Given air travel and the ease of viral transmission by asymptomatic or pre-symptomatic people, it was probably already too late for governments to expect border closures to be effective, but it was clear they would be happening. This was a time of terrifying uncertainty in the world. At AFS, the crisis team and I were bracing ourselves for the tsunami we knew was coming. What would be the plan for managing it?

LEADING IN CRISIS:

CHAPTER 4: The Crisis Management Toolkit

B y this stage, you've taken two important steps toward preparing for crisis management:

- you can identify the kind of crisis you are facing, and

- you can rapidly deploy a crisis team.

Your next step is to ensure that when a crisis hits, you can swiftly develop an effective plan to guide your team. As soon as a crisis appears, the crisis team leader and all other team members should turn to their Crisis Management Toolkit. This takes training, as impulse typically tells us to act first and search out tools later.

Everyone on the team should have a copy of the toolkit, in electronic and in hard-copy forms both inside and outside the office. When the power is out, or offices are inaccessible, alternate ways to locate the toolkit will be a lifesaver.

What should be in the toolkit? It should contain all the detail that can help the crisis team leader and other team members respond appropriately right from the start. A sample table of contents for a crisis management plan ends this chapter.

The toolkit serves three major purposes. First, it's an emergency action manual. Checklists are a great tool to allow team members to quickly perform vital functions like evaluating the level of crisis, activating the crisis team and determining team member roles. Checklists help flesh out the necessary steps for creating the crisis management plan, such as assigning tasks, establishing timelines, clarifying the decision-making process and managing follow-up. All crisis team members should have a checklist customized to that person's job inside the toolkit.

The second purpose of the toolkit is to ensure that communication can flow swiftly, accurately and adequately. This includes contact information for the range of stakeholders who may need to be reached immediately, as well as systems for getting information out to many parties at once.

In addition to all electronic communications tools, it can be invaluable to have a printout that lists information about contacts both at work and home, and not just a listing of links, emails or system usernames. Power may be out, or the internet down when you need to reach people quickly. Because contact information changes regularly, it's important to update the toolkit every six months, both in electronic and hard copy form.

The third purpose of the toolkit is to protect the safety and wellbeing of stakeholders and the organization. It should detail emergency resources, ranging from fire suppression to back-up systems and instructions for taking emergency action, at times when there are medical emergencies or other catastrophes, for example. It should also contain detail on how to protect the organization's reputation, such as how to work with the media spokesperson or outside public relations firm.

Good risk managers and good crisis managers hope for the best outcomes but are always scanning for trouble or threat before it appears. They are always thinking of strategies to surmount it and prioritizing action based on the best information available. The toolkit arms them with the material they need to respond.

For AFS, closing programs in China and Italy were Level 3 Full Impact crises.

No one knew exactly how the crisis would develop, but by March 12, 2020, the WHO declared Covid-19 to be a pandemic. On the same day, AFS International determined that for the safety and wellbeing of all participants, it would end all programs worldwide and return all participants home. AFS announced that decision publicly shortly thereafter.

In its 75-year history of participant exchange programs, AFS had never closed its worldwide operations. This was clearly a Level 4 Global Full Impact crisis, which for AFS meant I, as chief risk manager and general counsel, would take the lead. By March 16, as global repatriation work began, the crisis team at AFS International headquarters had grown from a small team of five for the earlier evacuations to a core crisis team of 12 to 15 (out of a total staff of fewer than 45).

It was immediately clear that this would be a marathon and that everyone needed a backup. Although AFS runs crisis trainings every year, the greatly expanded team meant many new members were untrained. This was our first challenge. Preparation is critical in a crisis, and in this case, our detailed existing crisis management toolkit saved the day. Every role had a quick-start checklist, along with a more detailed description. As the team grew, some members had to change roles. Within days, the crisis response included the entire AFS International staff. Fortunately, each person could read the applicable part of the toolkit and get to work, asking questions and learning on the job. The transitions proved seamless.

The next challenge was massive. It was to synchronize the work of the AFS International crisis team with the crisis teams of more than 55 AFS member organizations to ensure a coordinated response to communicate with all stakeholders and repatriate participants who were scattered all over the globe. We were fortunate that we all using the same framework so all the toolkits were in sync.

Key Takeways

- include everything the team needs to manage the crisis from the start

- keep the toolkit on paper and electronically in several locations; update contacts twice a year

- coordinate toolkits if you have affiliated organizations

Elements of a Crisis Management Plan

Table of Contents

—materials and business resumption resources

• What to do when contacted by the media

—training and media materials

4. Defining and assessing crises

    • How to determine if a crisis exists

    —handling a crisis vs. an emergency

    • How to determine the level of crisis

    —summary of crisis levels

    —crisis level evaluation checklist

5. Managing the crisis

    • Activate crisis response team based on the level of crisis

    • Share initial information with all concerned

    • Designate necessary resources to manage the crisis

    • Hold initial team meeting

    • Begin contacting necessary parties

    • Update and coordinate the response

6. Conducting a post-crisis evaluation

    • Hold a debriefing to assess what was learned

    —post-crisis evaluation worksheet

PART TWO. RESPONDING TO CRISIS— The AFS Level 4 Crisis Response

LEADING IN CRISIS:

CHAPTER 5: What to Do When a Crisis Arises

F or AFS, it was a daunting challenge to safely return more than 7,000 students from more than 70 countries to their more than 70 home countries in the midst of a pandemic. Exchanges do not simply operate back and forth from reciprocal countries. There were thousands of individual exchange pathways among countries in effect, each of which could require a complex travel path by plane, train and automobile.

The 1,200+ exchange pathways of AFS programs.

45

Repatriation was a global effort by thousands of staff and tens of thousands of volunteers. Managing that effort as borders were closing and flights were being cancelled worldwide required a carefully coordinated response and full-scale effort from the entire AFS global network. My job as crisis team leader became exponentially bigger.

How should a crisis team leader manage such a task? When any crisis hits, a crisis team leader should turn to the crisis management toolkit. There should be a specialty checklist that the crisis team leader can use to determine the action steps needed to manage the crisis and then bring it to a resolution, using input from each team member.

The crisis team leader checklist helps to create the basis for the plan the team must develop to respond effectively. It includes timelines for decision-making and for following up on information. It helps to determine who makes the decisions and who establishes communication plans.

As soon as AFS decided to close all programs and rank the pandemic a Level 4 Global Full-Impact Crisis, I immediately went to my checklist and began to act on each of the steps:

AFS Crisis Team Leader Checklist

1. Gather information and make an initial analysis of the situation. Establish the facts—what is known and what is not? What needs to be addressed immediately and what longer-term repercussions might emerge?

This requires clearly defining or framing the crisis as soon as possible. As things develop, the crisis team leader should constantly assess whether the crisis has changed, and reframe or redefine the crisis as needed, so that everyone remains clear on goals and objectives.

It is also critical that the crisis team leader ensures that everyone is working with the same information and that the information is accurate. This can be half the battle in crisis management. It was very challenging at the start of Covid-19.

2. Take immediate action as required. Determine what needs to be done to protect 1) people, 2) brand, 3) operations, and 4) property, and start taking those steps right away.

AFS's international headquarters are in New York City. By mid-March, New York was starting to see the first signs of a serious spread of the virus. On March 11, with only 269 cases of Covid-19 in the United States, AFS International began working remotely. On March 20, 2020, New York Governor Andrew Cuomo made the extraordinary decision to close all nonessential businesses.

3. Organize your team as appropriate. Now that you know more about the nature of the crisis, determine who the core team members should be. Does the crisis require an internal team member, an external team member or both? Is the documenter in place? Are specialists required? If so, alert them, even if you're not entirely sure yet how they will be needed. Team members should start by reviewing their own task checklists from the crisis toolkit.

Preparation is critical in a crisis, and in this case, AFS's detailed crisis management toolkit, especially the quick-start checklists, was invaluable in helping the team to quickly take shape and get to work. Team members used these critical tools, particularly when they changed roles as the team grew.

4. Ensure initial information is shared with all concerned. Disseminate the information that has been gathered and the steps that have been taken with all team members and all relevant stakeholders who are initially involved. This is an important opportunity to establish facts, keep information from becoming skewed or distorted, and establish confidence in the effort.

The crisis team leader can quickly establish a framework for how the team will work together and how often it will meet, clarifying roles and ensuring that all team members have the information and support they need.

The crisis team leader can also set the tone for effective teamwork by being calm, consistent and kind. Leadership matters in crises because crises can bring out the best or worst in people.

As we all experienced with the pandemic, getting accurate information about the virus, or even consistent responses from health authorities or governments was nearly impossible. For AFS, this made the external team member's job very taxing and, at the same time, vitally important. The external team member at AFS was responsible for gathering the necessary facts about the pandemic, air travel, border closings, government mandates, quarantines, etc. This information changed hourly and had to be disseminated rapidly and effectively to all AFS stakeholders.

That's where the internal team member came in. Her daunting job was to ensure that all external information was quickly and accurately shared with all stakeholders, to monitor and respond to social media, and also to support a vast flow of information from inside the organization on participant travel, organizational support, and public relations.

In some cases, ensuring that accurate information is shared with those who need it can be relatively straightforward. For AFS, under Covid-19, the effort proved to be almost surreal.

5. Review and organize communication channels. Establish who needs to be in the loop—customers, media, government entities, suppliers, insurers—by reviewing your stakeholder list. Determine which team member should contact each or receive inquiries from them. Determine how often updates should happen and then make sure they do. If there is information you don't yet have but are looking to get, let stakeholders know that.

As AFS began to execute its repatriation plan, it was clear that managing the flow of information from the top down and ground up would be potentially overwhelming. For every student traveling home, there was a host family, a sending family, a school, a local chapter, a national office, government embassies, and local staff and volunteers all of whom needed to come together to ensure safe travel and accurate information. The communications challenges were daunting. It was clear that traditional methods would be insufficient.

Almost immediately, the crisis team's internal team member created a group of 19 staff members who made what we termed "wave" calls every day to every AFS member organization in every country. This team met daily at 8 a.m. The internal team member then attended the daily 9 a.m. crisis team call to brief the rest of the crisis team on what these organizations' biggest concerns were, what questions they had, and what resources they needed to help them communicate with the vast network of affected stakeholders. The critical innovation of the wave call enabled the global leadership at AFS to align its work and communications with the actions and communications of each

AFS member office and each of its teams, and to support them and keep the process going forward.

These wave calls were vital, but then within days, most offices were closed, and staff were working remotely, creating even greater challenges. AFS responded as many other organizations did, by turning to videoconferencing. Although many people encountered videoconferencing for the first time during the pandemic, AFS was already very familiar with it, having begun using it six years earlier.

The AFS president and CEO held regular town hall videoconferences, with, at times, up to 200 of the core global leaders. Being able to hear and see each other on these videoconferences, share concerns and talk through options led to a number of course corrections as the crisis progressed, such as changing the timetable for each country's evacuation plans.

6. Make an in-depth analysis of the situation. Once the crisis team leader has addressed the most immediate needs, he or she should work with the team to determine the specifics of the plan for solving the crisis. Discuss what might be coming up next and ways to meet it. Concentrate on addressing the impact of the crisis, not just on managing the event that caused it. Bring in your team experts to help refine the options.

The top priority for AFS was and has always been to protect the safety and wellbeing of its stakeholders, with the most vulnerable coming first—in this case, the 15-to 18-year-old participants. While travel always presents risks, AFS believed it was far better for participants to be home with their families during a global pandemic, especially given the uncertainty about access to health care in host countries. The goal was first to bring participants home safely to their own families. If that could not be done safely or was not allowed, students would shelter in place, staying on program in the host country with their host families.

There were numerous challenges to bringing the participants home. Some travel routing became impossible as countries like the United States began limiting or eliminating through travel. At times, tickets were either astronomically priced or simply unavailable. AFS was working with dozens of travel agents and constantly relied on our outside travel risk advisors to assess all these travel possibilities and support a consistent approach.

Another hurdle for AFS was managing each country's requirements for quarantine on arrival. Many countries imposed self-quarantine rules, but others established quarantine facilities. Thailand put AFS participants up in a hotel in Bangkok. Where the sending AFS organization did not think the way the government planned to quarantine young returning AFSers was appropriate, participants sheltered in place with their host families.

Then came a new requirement from India. Our Indian participants hosted in Italy had to be tested and proven clear of Covid-19 before they could return home. However, it was nearly impossible to get asymptomatic people tested. And it took two weeks to get results, so participants had to stay in a hotel awaiting results, hoping a two-week-old test would satisfy immigration authorities in India.

7. Clarify the decision-making process. Determine who gets to decide the options for solving the crisis. Start with the most general decisions and move toward the specific. Focus on separating out interdependencies and breaking down the respective elements of decision-making. Anticipate what needs to be known or in place for decisions to be made, and then work to make sure those requirements can be met.

AFS is a decentralized, federated type of not-for-profit organization. The AFS network comprises more than 50 individual organizations or "members" located around the world.

Because each organization is independent (yet interdependent), decision-making can require significant coordination and consultation. AFS ramped up videoconferencing from 100,000 minutes a month before the crisis to more than one million minutes in the following month. A significant part of this time was spent ensuring everyone had the information needed for effective decision-making.

8. Establish timelines. When should decisions be implemented and in what order? How do these coordinate with planned updates and communication systems? What should be done if options don't move forward as planned?

In a more traditional crisis, establishing timelines would seem like a reasonable and fairly straightforward exercise. With Covid-19, it felt more like a white-water rafting expedition, confronted by unexpected obstacles that forced the constant adjustment of expectations and timelines.

While AFS was able to evacuate 80 percent of the participants within about two weeks, some could not return because their home country had closed its borders or travel was not possible. The timeline for their return was beyond the control of AFS.

With such a fluid crisis, two of the most important elements were 1) ensuring that each stakeholder was receiving the information needed (and not too much more), and 2) ensuring that AFS managed the expectations of those stakeholders effectively as external circumstances continued to change.

9. Coordinate the work of the group. Determine the output, meetings and progress reports expected of group members. The central role of the crisis team leader is to keep the crisis team on track. Often this can be straightforward, such as determining how often the team meets, setting the agenda, ensuring follow up and supporting team members. But Covid-19 was a different sort of crisis that required the entire AFS organization to continuously adapt to new information and personal challenges.

For the crisis management team, one early challenge was the vulnerability of our team to Covid-19. That meant being ready to replace members of the team immediately, if necessary. At the same time, the crisis was expanding in all directions, in magnitude, complexity, and intensity, so AFS had to radically ramp up the size of the team. The crisis team developed a hierarchy so that each core team member led another specialty team, while coordinating with crisis team members from all the other crisis teams in the AFS network.

Without realizing it at the time, I found myself constantly adapting team roles on the fly. I had to keep increasing the size of the team and putting people in charge of other teams that could bring information back to the crisis team or disseminate new policies, talking points or other information. At one point, one team member volunteered to prepare the agenda for each team call, which changed by the hour as the situation unfolded. This helped me tremendously by allowing me to focus on decision-making and next steps.

In an expanding crisis like Covid-19, it can be easy to lose sight of the big picture. It's extremely important for the crisis team leader to coordinate every aspect with the president or CEO and board leadership to ensure overall organizational alignment.

10. Monitor progress. Keep checking back with team members to make sure the crisis plan is on track and not derailed by misunderstanding, exhaustion or lack of coordination. Normally, this would be no more complex than monitoring progress of a team working on urgent business matters, but Covid-19 raised the bar.

For AFS, the communications requirements and complexity of repatriation were immense. At one point, I was receiving hundreds of emails, texts and calls an hour. It was impossible to keep up, regardless of our team structure and despite constant adjustments to make communications more efficient.

Within a few days, it was also clear that we had to make sure the crisis team and I were taking care of ourselves and each other. I made daily calls in the late afternoon with each core team member to check in.

By ensuring team members are not overstressed or too tired, you can help make sure your team functions at its best, avoiding inadvertent errors. Making avoidable mistakes in a crisis can derail a tremendous amount of good work, good will and risk mitigation. I followed the various team calls with a call to the AFS president to make sure the crisis team's work was in line with all the steps the president and international volunteer board of trustees were taking to manage the crisis.

Much of monitoring progress in a crisis like Covid-19 is grounded in effective, regular communication. At the same time, it is hard to overstate the importance of kindness, of showing appreciation and of being supportive. People can forget this critical aspect of teamwork when under high stress, but these are the most important times to keep them front and center in your thinking as a team leader.

11. Ensure ongoing communication flows inside and outside the team. Keep checking back to make sure stakeholders are receiving timely information about the way the crisis is being managed.

Covid-19 presented AFS with immense communications challenges. I held two crisis team meetings a day. Initially both focused on repatriation, but after about 10 days, with repatriation on track, the afternoon meeting shifted to strategy and alignment of the AFS network. AFS also convened regular executive team meetings, risk management team meetings, as well as legal, communications, public relations, and support staff meetings.

Innovations like the daily wave calls around the world organized by the internal team member helped tremendously. These calls, built on a tree-and-branch structure, allowed many people to quickly share information with others in an orderly way, which could then easily be shared with the crisis team.

AFS used all forms of technology where possible and constantly reorganized and refocused to be as efficient as possible. Our post-crisis evaluation showed that AFS mostly hit the mark—some stakeholders wanted a little less communication, some a little more, but the vast majority believed it was about right.

Communication was at the core of every action AFS took. Arranging travel for a single participant could require hundreds of calls and emails. Managing that level of detail without losing sight of the larger picture required a level of focus that only constant checking-in could maintain.

12. *Work toward de-escalating the crisis.* Even when the initial event that caused the crisis is over, continue to reel in the tendrils that may create trouble, particularly on the communications side.

Before attending law school, I worked as a carpenter. We had a saying that the first 90 percent of a job takes 90 percent of the time and the last 10 percent takes another 90. This applies equally to crisis management. At some point, the crisis starts to recede in intensity, but it isn't over. There are often dozens of issues remaining to be addressed, as well as post-crisis evaluations to conduct and lessons learned to be implemented.

Covid-19 has been a never-ending story of a crisis. For AFS, repatriation was 90 percent complete within weeks, but getting the last participants home took months. Other high school exchange organizations experienced this too. The impact of the virus on the student exchange industry has been vast and is still uncertain.

In any crisis, it is critical that the crisis team stay focused on the work ahead (except for post-crisis evaluations at appropriate times), especially in an ongoing crisis. It's rare for the crisis team to have to keep redefining its goals and objectives to such an extent, but that has been the case with this enduring crisis. Just like the finish work on a construction job, it's extremely important to finish the work, to keep assessing what remains to be done and to not let up until the job is done.

Key Takeaways

- consult checklists and respond quickly

- gather and share information, and maintain ongoing communication

- reassess the crisis and establish timelines for team actions

LEADING IN CRISIS:

CHAPTER 6: How to Manage an Evolving Crisis

The challenge with an evolving crisis like Covid-19 is that it keeps changing. The crisis team leader must continuously monitor the type of crisis the organization is facing and be prepared to adjust objectives and goals as circumstances change.

Managing an evolving crisis requires the team leader to focus on:

1. Clearly **defining or framing the crisis,** and regularly redefining and reevaluating the crisis as it changes.

2. **Communicating** clearly with the team and key stakeholders precisely what must be done or is being done to manage the crisis. This can change weekly, daily or even hourly.

3. **Carefully analyzing** the crisis with the best possible information so that resources are used most effectively, and changes are made to the plan as the situation evolves.

4. **Making rapid-fire decisions**, even with imperfect information.

Managing these four areas is only part of the crisis team leader's job, but in an evolving crisis it becomes vital. At the same time, crisis team leaders need to address self-care and support team members. (See chapters 12 and 13).

For many organizations, the first challenge of Covid-19 was to sort out how to work remotely. Many schools, businesses and governments found themselves utterly unprepared for such a radical change in approach.

AFS, however, was fully prepared for remote work, not only because it is a large multinational that works around the globe as a regular part of its business, but because after Hurricane Sandy in 2012, AFS had carefully evaluated how it would operate with no access to its New York headquarters. We had a plan, so shifting to remote work in a day was seamless.

For all of us though, Covid-19 evolved rapidly. The dramatic closure of the economy around the world and work-from-home orders for all but essential businesses meant that many organizations had to face immediate and potentially catastrophic financial consequences. Many people working from home also had children at home who needed care and attention. Many faced losing their jobs and sources of income. Millions and millions of people were suddenly furloughed or out of work, creating a cascading impact on other businesses.

These issues made Covid-19 very personal for crisis teams around the world. This is not always the case, but it added great complexity to this crisis. It meant that supporting each other, being kind to each other and talking through our concerns with each other was critical. Communications are always important in a crisis, but for an evolving crisis, the team also has to focus on itself, taking care of each other and helping hold each other up at different moments.

Managing Shifting Goals and Objectives

Governments responded differently around the world, though many provided Covid-19 stimulus funds through loans or grants. Many crisis teams had to divert energy immediately to cost-cutting measures and applying for funds.

At AFS, each member organization addressed these issues within its own national environment, but at AFS International headquarters, the president and the finance team, working with the board of trustees, had to develop a plan to cut costs dramatically and rapidly.

At the same time, the international crisis team and each AFS member organization had to maintain a laser focus on getting participants home safely. Large countries such as the United States stopped allowing through-travel, making it almost impossible to find a route home for some participants. Travel plans for each participant changed by the hour, taxing the organization as never before. For example, we had planned to return Argentine students home and evacuate those hosted there when Argentina closed its border without warning on March 15. As a result, these plans had to be canceled immediately, and arrangements made so that the participants, who fortunately were not already en route, remained in place with host families wherever they had been located.

This was rapid-fire decision-making in extraordinary times. The crisis team and I had to constantly develop policies and guiding principles to make travel decisions safely and equitably.

This rate of change created a new challenge for AFS. Our internal networks are set up to track each participant and share travel information as it is entered into the system. However, entering the data became impossible to manage because it changed so rapidly.

The AFS member offices weren't able to keep up with data entry for the travel plans for every participant. We found that sending and hosting numbers, which should be identical, weren't matching. We immediately added someone to help the AFS offices enter the data and work with the IT team to develop a way to quickly and transparently display all the information we needed, matching hosting and sending numbers and displaying snapshots for each AFS organization to track progress.

Within two weeks of announcing program closure, AFS had returned more than 5,000 of our 7,000 participants. Within three weeks, slightly more than 1,000 remained. We surpassed our own expectations.

Key Takeaways

- clearly define and redefining the crisis, goals and objectives

- commit to making data-driven decisions where possible

- be decisive

CHAPTER 7: Protecting Your Most Important Assets in a Crisis

C rises require decisions about priorities. We know intuitively that if we had to suddenly evacuate our home, we would get the family and pets out first, and hope we remember to grab the "go" bag. Maybe after that, we would rescue family photos or mementos.

With businesses. it's critical to approach crises in a similar way—to preserve what is most important first. Then as you get a handle on the crisis, minimize the impact through thoughtful analysis, careful action and clear, accurate communications.

What is most important? We all have our core values and goals. For mission-driven organizations, there is nothing more essential than protecting your ability to deliver on your mission. In a crisis, you need to deal with the immediate issues while focusing on how the crisis might affect not only your mission but also your brand, your goals and ultimately, your organization's survival.

Aligning with Your Mission and Core Values

How do you know that you're making the right decisions during a crisis? One approach is to keep your crisis response aligned with your mission and core values. All organizations have these, whether they operate for profit or not. Your goal should be not just to end the crisis, but also to bring it to resolution in keeping with the principles of your brand, aligning with your mission.

If your business produces a product or service of a certain quality, make sure the decisions that are part of your crisis response mirror your standards and values and reflect your brand. If your product involves a lot of information, for example, your crisis response should also. If your business is highly personal, your response should be as well.

In an organization with the size and geographic diversity of AFS, maintaining core values across the network during the crisis meant dealing with a host of structural, geographic, language and time differences. AFS member organizations have both volunteer boards and paid staff, so governance in a crisis can be difficult. One immediate challenge for AFS was to ensure that the crisis team leader in each country was aligned with the rest of the leadership in that organization. Another challenge was ensuring that the international headquarters was fully aligned with each of the AFS member organizations.

A critical role for the president at AFS has always been to ensure coordination with all the other AFS organizations around the world on all the essential steps required for long-term survival and growth. Any organization that operates with entities that have a role in providing its products or services must ensure alignment in decision-making. When everyone uses this approach, decisions can flow more easily.

Working closely with the finance team and the volunteer board of trustees, the president had to rapidly develop plans for recovery of global operations. Using scenario planning for the future of the entire AFS network, he had to ensure that key decisions that required approval of the board could be made quickly with adequate information, consultation and deliberation.

The best way to help ensure alignment is to ground decision-making and communications in the mission and values of the organization. That means carefully considering every decision to see if it aligns with core values. This helps everyone hew to the larger picture and protects the brand. Ensuring alignment in an organization as widespread and diverse as AFS also meant constantly reaching out to all the stakeholder groups regularly, clearly framing the goals and actions needed for each group. (See the next chapter for more on this.)

Covid-19 has given us all an opportunity to reassess what is important and to protect that. This crisis forced us to try new ways to respond by putting our core values first. Some worked better than others, and some have now permanently become part of our organization's way of doing business.

As crisis team leader, I knew that getting participants home safely and protecting those sheltering in place were the most important and were critical to the brand and mission of AFS. That's how we allocated our resources to meet the challenges we were facing. We have always put participant safety first and there is no more essential time to stay focused on that than in a crisis like Covid-19. I also tried to do all I could to manage repatriation without taking up too much of the president's or the board's time because I knew they were looking ahead to the implications for AFS.

Protecting Your Brand in a Crisis

Good crisis leadership is the best tool you have in a crisis to protect your brand, your reputation and your business goodwill. Why? Because these are intangible assets that can't be insured.

Insurance is a fine tool for protecting tangible assets, like real estate, cash, vehicles and inventory. A tangible asset can be readily valued. Insurance companies can reimburse the value when there is a covered loss of property, like a fire, theft or supply chain break. Preserving these can be essential. But some of the most important assets of any organization are intangible—such as goodwill and its reputation. Those can be lost in a crisis, too.

Unfortunately, you can't create an insurable value or properly make an insurance claim for the loss of your good business reputation, even though that is one of your most important assets. The value of your brand can't be insured. Public perception about the liability and practices of your organization is primarily what drives your reputation and brand, not legal or financial outcomes.

The Tylenol tampering case demonstrates a response to a crisis that aligns with brand and reputation. Tylenol was one of the most trusted brands in 1982 when someone laced a number of containers with cyanide, repackaged them and put them on the shelf at drugstores in the Chicago area. A number of people died as a result.

Johnson & Johnson, makers of Tylenol, immediately asked its team: "How do we protect the people?" and "How do we save the product?" These two questions drove its response—notifying the public immediately of the risk, removing all containers from the shelves and stopping production. In the end, the Tylenol brand came back stronger because it aligned its crisis response with its core values and customers recognized that.

How well does insurance protect what is important? Insurance is a major risk management tool, but has limitations:

1. It can only come into play after a big loss and reputational or brand damage may already have occurred.

2. It can only protect an asset that is insurable.

3. It only protects assets that are adequately and specifically insured.

During the Covid-19 crisis, many organizations turned to their insurance policies with hopes for coverage under the Business Interruption benefit. Their businesses had been interrupted by government shutdown orders, many to the point of near bankruptcy, and they badly needed funds to resuscitate them.

However, few Business Interruption policies responded to the risk of pandemic. Business Interruption typically comes into play when there has been actual physical damage that stops the flow of business, like a tree that falls on a roof. While business had certainly been interrupted for countless organizations, court ruling after court ruling held that the virus was not a trigger for coverage under typical insurance policies.

Some of the very biggest risks—pandemics, wars, nuclear accidents—are not covered by insurance companies. The scale of these risks can be so vast that insurers can't properly evaluate or rate the risk. For some of the very biggest crises, insurance may not be a savior, even for the protection of physical assets.

To protect your most important assets, good crisis leadership is the tool that fills the big spaces insurance can't cover. You can rely on it even more fully than on insurance.

Key Takeaways

- brand value and reputation are uninsurable and can be lost in a moment

- align your crisis response to your values and mission to protect your brand

- only effective leadership can save intangible assets in a crisis

CHAPTER 8: Managing Expectations in a Crisis

To manage stakeholder expectations, the first step is to know what those expectations are. Depending on your brand and the type of crisis, they could vary widely. Is it acknowledgment? Apology? Transparency? Direction? Attention? Empathy? Effort? A way to make it right? A promise to stop what is allegedly causing the problem? Or is it continued performance no matter what? Delivering on brand expectation may feel overwhelming in a crisis, but you will be able to deliver on at least some parts of it.

We deal with managing expectations at length in our book, *No Complaints, No Lawsuits*, but it's worth reflecting on how people and organizations effectively manage expectations in a crisis. Sometimes people have totally unrealistic expectations, other times they may be quite high but still reasonable.

For example, AFS sent thousands of participants on an international program. AFS believed that it was reasonable for participants to expect AFS to help them find a way to get home safely in a pandemic. It's also totally understandable that students would be unhappy to have their programs cut short.

To manage expectations in a crisis, first look at each stakeholder group. In the case of AFS, stakeholders include participants, sending parents, hosting parents, volunteers, staff, schools and governments. Each had expectations about what AFS should be doing. The AFS crisis team had to find a way to ensure close communications with each stakeholder group to understand these expectations. Once you are aware of each expectation, you have three options:

1) Meet the expectation

2) Change the expectation (then meet the new one)

3) Don't meet the expectation.

Meeting expectations is important, because satisfied people tend not to complain or sue, helping protect your organization's brand, resources and reputation.

The first step is to figure out which stakeholder expectations you can meet, declare them and meet them. Then, let your stakeholders know what expectations you won't be able to meet because of the crisis. Acknowledge shortcomings that may not be in keeping with your mission and principles, explain what you are doing to correct them and keep working to address these shortcomings.

Be mindful of how wildly different expectations can be. Everyone has experienced Covid-19 differently, making managing their expectations particularly difficult. For example, as AFS was trying to bring home its Turkish participants from around the world, the Turkish government declared that all participants would be quarantined on a military base for two weeks after arrival. The crisis team and I determined, working with the team in Turkey, that this was not in the best interests of our participants' safety and wellbeing since they are minors. AFS decided to let them shelter in place until things settled down. We informed the participants, the sending parents and other key stakeholders so everyone understood why AFS was taking this action for this specific group.

Staying true to the brand is a major tool of reputational risk management. You may find there is more forgiveness out there than you think, as long as your actions hew to your business principles. Conversely, failing to do this can explain why some stakeholders are dissatisfied even after you feel you've been able to gain good control over a crisis. A crisis is an opportunity to expose your mission to the world. Don't just repeat your mission in public statements, demonstrate how your business is guided by it.

For AFS, we knew our participants would be extremely disappointed to have their exchange experiences end abruptly. They expected a full exchange program, some lasting for a full academic year, which we knew we could not deliver. At the same time, some participants had to shelter in place with host families even though schools had closed. That was also not what these participants or their parents expected.

We knew we could not meet those expectations, so we put a small team to work to adapt an online skills-building course called the Global Competence Certificate to meet these participants' needs.

AFS had to roll the program out rapidly and immediately ensure there were some 80 trained facilitators to run it and its online forums. These forums had to be linked with support staff around the world so any potential issues, such as distressed participants, could be channeled to the appropriate support staff in each country. It proved invaluable in helping the students process their experience, providing them with a sense of community and a place to share what they were going through.

One respondent commented: "I would like to thank AFS for this GCC program. It took me a while to finish because I was in denial for a pretty long time. But being involved with this actually helped me move on. Reading the comments on the forum and communicating with others through live sessions reminded me of why I wanted to be an exchange student in the first place, and how I'm actually not alone. I'd like to say that being a part of the AFS community is a great honor."

This was just one example of how AFS adjusted expectations it could not meet and then created expectations it could meet, consistent with its brand and mission. In any crisis, preparation is critical to success. However, once the crisis hits, successfully managing it requires anticipating what's coming, adapting plans and reallocating resources.

It is just as important to keep an eye on the horizon to see what's coming as it is to pay attention to the waves crashing over the walls or the cracks in the road beneath your feet. This ability to anticipate, adjust and adapt was especially important with Covid-19 because its impact has been vast, hitting every part of the world and all sectors of the economy. This cascading effect meant that our solid plan at 9 a.m. often required radical adjustment by 3 p.m. the same day.

Key Takeaways

- consider all stakeholders' expectations and meet, change or make clear why you can't meet them

- communicate regularly with each stakeholder; don't forget social media and PR

- manage stakeholders expectations in line with your values

LEADING IN CRISIS:

CHAPTER 9: Managing Communications with Stakeholders

In times of crisis, people want to know that you care more than they care what you know. —**Will Rogers, American humorist and entertainer**

O ne of the most important aspects of crisis management is having clear roles and responsibilities and clear lines of communication. This avoids confusion and duplication of effort, promoting the most efficient use of resources. So much of crisis management is about communicating effectively and establishing clear roles to ensure clear, consistent messaging.

AFS's quick-start checklists for each team member contain a one-page job description that delineates clear roles among traditional crisis team members. When team members don't contradict or override each other, stakeholders will have confidence in what they hear from the team.

One unique challenge for AFS was getting everyone aligned and in agreement on the critical next steps of each phase of AFS's plans. This was initially perplexing, until we realized that while people in one country were in crisis because of Covid-19, overwhelmed with suffering and death, others had not yet experienced a single case.

This aspect of the crisis led to wildly different experiences and perspectives for every person in every city, in every country, in all different socioeconomic situations. It affected people's perceptions of what was real. We knew we had to do a better job of listening to each other and communicating effectively.

We realized the most effective tool to create alignment for a vastly diverse crisis response tailored to multiple realities was a forum for large groups around the world to see and hear from each other regularly. It was, in all likelihood, those million minutes a month on videoconference calls that made the difference and helped us all support each other, despite the differences in our personal circumstances.

Communicating with Stakeholders

It is easy to focus on customers and forget all the other people affected by the decisions you make, especially in a crisis. Be sure to consider the full range of stakeholders affected by the crisis. Consult the stakeholder diagram in chapter 1. Which of these apply to you? Who might be upset, angry or experiencing loss, whether or not you feel their response is justified?

Carefully considering the position of stakeholders is not the same as admitting fault or blame. Sometimes organizations ignore complaints or arguments when they believe allegations against them are untrue or unjustified. This is a mistake. Stakeholder anger and misunderstanding should be addressed proactively as it can create a crisis all on its own, often magnified by social media.

Not-for-profits and mission-driven organizations like AFS often rely on a wide variety of stakeholders: paid staff, volunteers, collaborative partners, such as schools or nongovernmental organizations, governmental agencies and third-party service providers (such as transportation companies, consultants and independent contractors). For-profit organizations are highly sensitive to the temperament of investors. All organizations rely on good relationships with donors, funders or financial institutions, industry peers and the media. The distinctions between stakeholder groups can be blurry, but it's extremely important to know they are there and to ensure that you can reach them.

AFS found regular videoconference calls helped align global leadership, both volunteers and staff. Daily wave calls with other AFS offices helped align crisis teams and support staff. Daily online posts on actions and resources helped disseminate information to AFS's stakeholders. Internal participant support portals helped ensure that timely information on the status of each participant was shared as needed. Regional calls with volunteer groups helped ensure that volunteers were heard and were aligned with AFS's actions. We developed talking points almost daily, posting them on websites and social media to ensure consistent messaging. All these steps were aimed at reaching all key stakeholders, both to listen to their needs and concerns and to share vital information about how AFS was managing the crisis.

Another example of reaching out to stakeholders is described in the article from *La Gaceta* in Argentina about AFS repatriation efforts there.

TUCUMÁN. They will never forget it. It was the trip of a lifetime: living with a different family in a new school, a different culture and a language that was not Spanish. But the pandemic forced them to leave those countries without time to say goodbye to everyone, to undertake a return that was an odyssey. With flights canceled without notice, borders closed to passage and uncertainty around the world, the organization American Field Service (AFS Intercultural Programs) managed to repatriate 12 boys hosted in Tucumán to their home country safe and sound.

A week before the WHO declared the pandemic, the cultural exchange organization decided to suspend all its programs and start an evacuation process for its participants. AFS had 7,500 teens, ages 15–17, scattered around the world. Among them were 200 Argentines and 400 foreigners in our country. From Tucumán, there were five boys in Italy, five in the United States, one in England and the other in Indonesia. Juan Médici, AFS executive director for Argentina, Uruguay and Brazil, talked with *La Gaceta*, along with Mitch Thibaud, director of institutional relations.

"Every day meant finding a solution to many obstacles. During the crisis, our main objective was to ensure the wellbeing of the participants and give support to the children and parents. One of the most difficult things was explaining to parents what was going on when no one knew at the time and telling them why we had made certain decisions. At first, they thought we were exaggerating about total evacuation. But we received information from organizations we consulted that warned us that a health tsunami was coming. Now they understand and are grateful, but in those moments, it was difficult. Children had to be removed from safe places—the families where they were, to be transferred at a time when governments began to restrict movement. A tremendous logistical process had to be carried out," Médici said.

https://www.lagacetasalta.com.ar/nota/140289/actualidad/odisea-12-adolescentes-repatriados-estaban-viaje-intercambio-otros-paises.html

This example also shows how important it is to be attentive to public relations communications, particularly for Level 3 and 4 crises. You can be sure that crisis information you provide internally in these cases will find its way to the outside world unless your external messaging is adequate. Ensure that your website and social media are up-to-date and aligned with all other messaging. This is critical to overall communications effectiveness.

Managing external messaging is an important role for your media team member. The key tools in communicating with stakeholders are to speak with integrity and to report reliably and regularly. Designate someone to speak to the media who can be a source of trusted detail and channel all information through that person. Provide the kind of information you would want to hear if you were a stakeholder.

If you don't know the status of a situation, say so, rather than offering speculative information. Don't be silent. Instead, let your stakeholders know right away that you are working to address the crisis. Let them know when they can expect to hear from you next, even if there is still no new information to offer at that time. This will help tremendously to bolster their confidence in your leadership and your crisis team.

The internal team member on our crisis team held daily calls with our public relations firm to discuss messaging on more than 50 websites, drafting public statements and responses to articles being written about AFS and addressing countless social media posts. We knew that consistent messaging was critical to protecting the brand. Many participants and their parents were understandably upset that the exchange experience was being cut short. Explaining AFS's assessment of why this was safest for participants and providing regular support throughout the process required monitoring and responding to social media activity all over the world.

The Compassionate Response

When communicating with stakeholders, especially in a crisis, the value of a compassionate response cannot be overstated.

We talk about the compassionate response in our book *No Complaints, No Lawsuits.* It is one of our guiding risk management principles and an invaluable tool to protect brand and reputation, especially when the potential damage to others is significant.

in the past, some businesses would close off the world when they found themselves in the midst of a crisis in hopes of avoiding more liability. The spokesperson might respond to questions with, "no comment", or "talk to our lawyer," Little was offered when it came to reaching out to those most affected by the crisis.

This kind of response generally exacerbates the crisis. When things go wrong, most people want to be treated with compassion, not ignored, and certainly not treated with disdain. One of the surprising things we've found about managing the risk of complaints and lawsuits is that people don't necessarily sue or complain because something terrible happened. It's often because they are angry or upset at the way they were treated, or the poor way they felt a matter was handled.

People want to be heard and treated with respect and empathy, particularly when they are involved in a crisis they consider to be of your making or within your control to manage. Whether you think their feelings are justified or not, consider ways to respond that are supportive of people who feel they have had a bad experience.

Train your staff and stakeholders not to discuss liability, make promises, or speculate when they are dealing with a crisis. But encourage them to be personal and show they care. There is a big difference between saying "we care about what happened" and "we are at fault." It's possible to be compassionate without increasing liability.

A surprising outcome is that it's also possible for an organization's reputation to grow as a result of its compassion in managing a loss or crisis. You may not have been able to prevent what happened, but you can contribute greatly to what happens afterwards.

The time for the compassionate response is often immediately at the start of a crisis, when everyone is first trying to understand what has happened. Typically, the decision to respond with generosity and care, even before all the issues are clear, needs to come straight from the leadership. This sets the tone for the way the crisis will continue to unfold.

Key Takeaways

- take the time to Identify *all* your stakeholders

- develop a communications plan as quickly as possible that allows you to listen to your stakeholders and share key information with all of them

- build compassion into your response

LEADING IN CRISIS:

PART THREE.
LEADING IN CRISIS

LEADING IN CRISIS:

CHAPTER 10: How to Manage an Enduring Crisis

"It is better to light a candle than to curse the darkness."—
Author Unknown

For many crises, the crisis management team is not also personally dealing with the crisis and can expect that, regardless, an end is in sight. Typically, at some point, the events and problems begin to resolve, and seemingly endless hours diminish. Regular life resumes, albeit sometimes differently.

Covid-19 has been one of those rare crises that have deeply affected us all in ways we didn't foresee: it has been global, evolving, and enduring, making it unique in three ways:

1. It affects everyone at once, though in different ways.

2. It evolves over time.

3. It seems to be endless.

It's fortunately rare to find this perfect storm of a crisis, but it is important to analyze carefully how to manage it. As the world becomes more complex and interconnected, we need to be prepared for more crises like this one.

In chapter 6, we looked at how to manage an evolving crisis. Here the focus is on how to manage a crisis that never seems to end. To fully understand how Covid-19 has affected us all and our ability to respond, we turn to what we can learn from two famous enduring crises that seemed to have no end in sight.

The Spanish Flu of 1918

The closest comparison to the Covid-19 crisis is probably the Spanish Flu. Like Covid-19, this pandemic lasted far too long. It began in February 1918 and wasn't over until April 1920—an enduring crisis. We rarely read about it because it was such a challenging time that once it was over, no one wanted to talk about it.

The Spanish Flu infected at least 500 million people–about a third of the world's population at the time. It occurred in four successive waves, killing up to 50 million people, making it one of the deadliest pandemics in human history. The first recorded infection was in Fort Riley, Kansas on March 4, 1918, but because of WWI, the news was suppressed. Spain, being neutral, openly reported its cases, which is why the illness became known as the Spanish Flu.

In the United States, the response to the first wave of the pandemic was the same as the response we saw to Covid-19—largely local, varying from state to state. Measures used to combat the flu included requiring people to wear masks in public and closing schools and places of public entertainment.

Though most people complied, some complained the masks were uncomfortable or cut holes in them to smoke. Masks in 1918, however, were merely gauze and may have been significantly less effective than today's more substantive ones. There were campaigns to shame people into wearing masks. Like today, many people claimed being required to wear them infringed on their civil liberties.

Just as WWI was ending, a second wave began. Unfortunately, people were by then much more resistant to wearing masks. In San Francisco people formed an Anti-Mask League. One person was shot and killed for not wearing a mask.

It seems clear though that cities that enforced stricter rules for a longer period of time were able to flatten the rate of infection. Nevertheless, the second wave was far deadlier than the first, apparently because the virus had mutated and become more lethal. Wartime troop movements near the end of the war exacerbated the dangerous situation. The inability to quarantine (due to the war) and a shortage of healthcare workers contributed to mortality rates. In those days, tools to develop a vaccine did not exist.

It's easy to find parallels to today's pandemic and to see the challenges we all face with a crisis that goes on and on. We see that people can endure quarantine for only so long before quarantine fatigue sets in and people take risks they would not have at the onset. One of the hallmarks of an enduring crisis is the challenge of continuing to lead long after the team or the stakeholders are exhausted.

A certain visionary persistence is critical to managing such a long crisis. With the Spanish Flu, it is clear that more leadership energy was directed to the war effort than to combating the pandemic. This meant that before it was all over, more people died of the Spanish Flu than from the war.

The Shackleton Expedition

Sir Ernest Shackleton

A classic example of the leadership requirements for managing an enduring and extreme crisis is the Antarctic expedition led by Sir Ernest Shackleton from 1914 to 1917. Because the team of explorers was totally on its own and circumstances were dire, the leadership decisions Shackleton made can be more easily identified and evaluated than the complex and diverse responses to the Spanish Flu.

Ernest Shackleton was an Irish-born English explorer who set off from England in August 1914 with a crew of 27 on a three-masted ship aptly named the *Endurance*. His initial mission was to be the first to cross Antarctica via the South Pole. In January 1915, the crew came within sight of Antarctica, but pack ice prevented them from getting close enough to land. As temperatures became colder, the ship itself became trapped in the ice and was unable to move.

Suddenly, Shackleton's mission changed to one of survival. The crew struggled to cut the ship free of the ice, but temperatures kept dropping and the effort proved fruitless. Shackleton realized they would have to wait out the winter aboard the ship. He feared boredom, idleness and dissent more than the ice and bitter cold. He knew that keeping morale high was critical to surviving the winter.

To combat this, he maintained daily routines, like swabbing the deck, collecting specimens and hunting for seals and penguins. He also made sure to celebrate each small daily success. He kept a calendar of important dates and made sure his men celebrated the holidays they would have at home. He even created a football field on the ice where the men could get some exercise and break the monotony.

Shackleton and his crew playing on a frozen football pitch.

Shackleton and his crew remained on the trapped ship for eight months, until October 27, 1915. Unfortunately, before the summer temperatures in the Southern Hemisphere warmed enough to potentially free the ship, it began leaking. Ultimately, the *Endurance* was crushed by the intense pressure created by the freezing and shifting sea ice.

Forced to abandoned ship, Shackleton and his crew were left marooned on the ice, miles and miles from any potential rescue, with three small lifeboats, several tents and some supplies. Almost immediately, Shackleton announced a new goal: "Ship and stores have gone, so now we'll go home." They then began an arduous trek for survival, dragging their heavy lifeboats and supplies over the ice.

Endurance stuck in the ice.

Shackleton realized he had to embody the new mission of survival, to exude optimism, courage and confidence. But as Andrew Little said in the December 24, 2011 *New York Times* article by Nancy Koehn: "The hardest part of leadership is not just feeding your team with ideas and motivation but feeding yourself. In the face of enormous obstacles, Shackleton found a way to do this." He continued to keep the men's focus on the future and to take every step he could to avoid pessimism and anxiety among the crew.

By April 1916, they had progressed to a point where the ice began to break up, so the crew then boarded their lifeboats. A week later, they landed on the desolate, barren and rocky Elephant Island. It was their first time on land in two years.

Launching the James Caird.

Shackleton immediately started planning his next moves. He knew his crew could not survive on Elephant Island. With five crew members, he embarked on an 800-mile journey in a 22-foot lifeboat named the *James Caird*, managing to guide the boat to South Georgia Island. The journey took 17 days over open water and freezing weather through turbulent seas so high they were forced to hold the sextant up between the troughs of the high waves to get their bearings. Once they reached South Georgia, however, they realized they were on the opposite side of the island from any settlement. They then had to hike for many hours, climbing high peaks and crossing large ice fields–a feat never before accomplished there–before miraculously reaching a whaling outpost on the other side of the island.

Over the next few months, Shackleton set sail in three different ships to return to Elephant Island to rescue his remaining crew. At first, no ship could cut through the ice. Finally, on August 30, 1916, aboard a Chilean steamer, he was finally able to rescue the remaining 22 men.

Celebrating Shackleton's return to Elephant Island.

"I have done it," he wrote "Not a life lost, and we have been through hell."

His and their story is one for the ages.

Author Michael Smith observed in his article, "What Made Shackleton a Great Leader?" "He was an inspiration who instilled a belief that the marooned men would survive and get home.

"Shackleton instinctively understood the importance of teamwork and threw a protective cloak around his men. All were treated equally, and he took particular care of anyone struggling to cope. He made each person feel as though they were as important as the next and there were no favorites. Scientists shared the same chores with sailors and sailors helped take scientific readings. When the winter clothing was distributed, Shackleton ensured the crew were supplied before the officers. During one horrendous journey, he gave his mittens to a desperate colleague." (Smith, https://shackletonlondon.com/blogs/articles/shackleton-great-leader)

These are some of the key qualities, behaviors and actions that a crisis management leader must demonstrate to maximize the chance of a positive outcome to a crisis, especially an enduring one. We would refer to these as modeling compassion, inspiring trust and confidence, actively listening and taking care of the team.

In her *New York Times* piece, "Leadership Lessons from the Shackleton Expedition," author Koehn wrote, "I was struck by Shackleton's ability to respond to constantly changing conditions. He had begun the voyage with a mission of exploration, but it quickly became a mission of survival." (Koehn, Dec. 24, 2011)

Smith writes, "He was also good at improvisation, a man not afraid to throw away the rulebook or abandon plans if they were not working."

Also important, Shackleton delegated well. He put Frank Wild in charge of the men remaining on Elephant Island. Wild did an incredible job maintaining morale and keeping the survivors there fed and alive through months of uncertainty over whether Shackleton had even reached his destination. Selecting the right people and building an effective leadership team are critical for success.

Koehn also wrote, "When a few men expressed skepticism about [Shackleton's] plans, he acted quickly to contain their opposition and negativity by trying to win them over and keeping close watch on them. He assigned several potential troublemakers to his own tent on the ice, proving the value of the adage, 'Keep your friends close and your enemies closer.'"

Shackleton demonstrated the kind of leadership required today. He inspired his team, he showed humility by offering his mittens to another and ensuring the crew had winter clothing before the officers. He held to his values, that he would get everyone home safely, and he was confident he would succeed despite many setbacks. He supported the crew and boosted team morale. He created an atmosphere of collaboration. He kept an eye out for conflict and made himself visible to the skeptics.

Shackleton was decisive, yet flexible, not losing sight of the big picture. He showed compassion and managed to take care of himself and his team. He built a strong team and delegated responsibility well when he departed from Elephant Island to seek help. And he never stopped looking for the next opportunity.

What most fully determines the outcome of an enduring crisis? The examples of the Shackleton Expedition, the Spanish Flu and Covid-19 demonstrate that leadership is essential to effectively managing a crisis that endures. In these cases, it can be a matter of life and death.

CHAPTER 11: New Leaders for a New World

Our leadership approach in turbulent times needs to be less command and control, more empathetic, to empower others, to listen to them, to communicate frequently and clearly. We need to be honest and transparent as the information changes; we need rapid feedback loops as we experiment with solutions. —Helena Morrisey, American financier, author

Tomás Chamorro-Premuzic notes in his *Forbes Magazine* article, "Why are Some Leaders Better than Others in a Crisis," that the most critical leadership traits in a crisis are intelligence, accurate threat sensitivity, integrity, and trustworthiness (Chamorro-Premuzic, March 15, 2020). Strong analytical thinking and the ability to anticipate what may be coming are also critical. These are all traits that are either inherent or developed and earned over time through experience and thoughtful reflection.

We would expect effective leaders to demonstrate these qualities and traits in normal situations. But not every leader can be an effective leader in a crisis. Not everyone is cut out to be an

Ernest Shackleton. In a crisis, some can become so enveloped in the situation and stressed themselves that they fall prey to fears or pessimism and no longer reflect the qualities that help hold a team together.

In other words, crisis leadership is not the same as corporate leadership or leadership in general. Not only do evolving and enduring crises require a different skill set, but crisis leaders must ensure their teams work at their optimal level. At the same time, crisis leaders must take care of themselves so that they, too, are thinking clearly and working at their best.

Leaders today need to be unpretentious, have empathy, and value diversity. Today's effective leaders are coaches and collaborators who will do what it takes to ensure their team members have what they need to be and do their best. Leadership qualities like calmness, confidence, compassion, consistency, kindness, transparency, honesty, courage, optimism and respect are critical to building trust.

Leaders are also most effective when they are genuine. Authentic leaders know their strengths and weaknesses. This self-awareness improves communications and builds stronger relationships, critical in a crisis. Today's leaders need the integrity that comes from aligning thoughts and actions with values.

Leading during Covid-19 has required making decisions without adequate information. This is frustrating and slightly terrifying and was one of the toughest aspects at AFS of managing participants' repatriation. One small but poignant example was whether participants should wear masks while traveling home.

On Feb. 29, U.S. Surgeon General Dr. Jerome Adams tweeted, "masks do not offer any benefit to the average citizen… They are NOT effective in preventing (the) general public from catching #Coronavirus"

The WHO also raised concerns about wearing masks, citing a potential false sense of security. The CDC and the European CDC also indicated early on that masks were ineffective. A month later, the CDC began recommending cloth masks, citing them as important to combat rapid virus transmission across the United States.

We now know from a recent study published in the *Lancet Medical Journal* that masks reduce the risk of infection approximately fivefold.

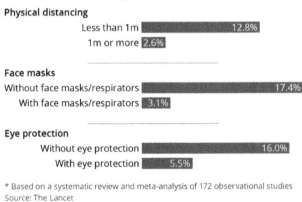

Face Masks & Distancing Reduce COVID-19 Risk

Chance of COVID-19 transmission based on the following scenarios*

Physical distancing

Less than 1m — 12.8%
1m or more — 2.6%

Face masks

Without face masks/respirators — 17.4%
With face masks/respirators — 3.1%

Eye protection

Without eye protection — 16.0%
With eye protection — 5.5%

* Based on a systematic review and meta-analysis of 172 observational studies
Source: The Lancet

statista

However, during repatriation, AFS had to decide whether to secure masks for traveling participants. We relied on our external team member (see chapter 3) to research this. He quickly saw masks weren't recommended and scientists hadn't reached a consensus. But we also listened to our staff in China and Hong Kong, where wearing masks was already more common. They urged us to locate and use masks where we could.

We decided to advise staff that traveling participants use masks when possible, but to recognize that countries held differing views and that masks might not be available. Some decisions must be made without reliable data, but active listening helps. We listened to our colleagues in China and Hong Kong, who had experience with Covid-19. We went with their experience because we had established rapport and trust.

CHAPTER 12: How Effective Leaders Inspire Team Success

O ne thing we now know from living with the Covid-19 pandemic is that everyone has to manage this crisis and the challenges that come with it, from parents with kids no longer attending school to schoolteachers to CEOs of the largest companies. Crisis leaders during this pandemic experienced the crisis in myriad ways at once—personally and professionally—as did their team members.

To be effective crisis managers in this situation, we need an effective team, and trust must be at the core. A team that trusts each other is a team that can operate at an optimal level over a long period of time, especially in an enduring crisis.

Even the most seasoned leaders can watch leadership skills evaporate as a crisis batters them. They can forget their actions speak loudest; that how they behave is central to the success of the entire effort. In this chapter, we assess what effective leaders *do*; their behaviors and actions in managing an enduring crisis as it unfolds.

1. Build Trust

A team is not a group of people that work together. A team is a group of people that trust each other. —**Simon Sinek, British-American author and motivational speaker**

Crisis team leaders need to inspire more than to drive. To inspire, a leader must be trusted. Trust is built by the actions described in this chapter—taking the time to get to know each person on your team, always speaking the truth, sharing credit and accepting blame, listening actively, leading by example, being consistent and fair and keeping promises. To create alignment in a crisis, to ensure everyone is working together as effectively as possible, leaders must build trust with their key stakeholders.

A person's title can instill trust, but that doesn't carry weight over time if actions are weak, ineffective or inconsistent. Experience and the ability to stay calm helps.

As we worked through the uncharted waters of Covid-19, we were all buffeted about daily, at times by our own struggles. It became imperative to build and maintain trust to get through the many hardships of the crisis. One thing Covid-19 made clear: crises that require diverse teams and intense and vast coordination need leaders who can inspire the trust their team will use to lead others.

Key Takeaways

- Build trust to create a high-performing team

- Lead by example

- Share credit and accept blame

2. Communicate Effectively

To effectively communicate, we must realize that we are all different in the way we perceive the world and use this understanding as a guide to our communication with others.— **Anthony Robbins, American motivational speaker**

Crisis leaders must know the core elements of effective communication—body language, tone, humor, positive feedback, active listening, openness and focus. But they must also be aware that people's experiences may be very different. People involved in the same crisis can perceive it differently and may be going through their own crises. Any team leader trying to manage the Covid-19 crisis on a global level had to realize this quickly.

Value Diversity

Our stakeholders are in different time zones across the globe, they are from different cultures, they speak different languages, and most important, they experienced Covid-19 in vastly different ways. To manage this, AFS activated its international crisis team. Each team member had a specific role and each led a team of others supporting the overall effort and coordinating with crisis teams around the world in this Level 4 Full Global Impact crisis.

From the onset, we had thousands of conversations, calls, videoconferences, emails and texts. Some places had no Covid-19 cases and didn't expect them; others, like Italy and China, went through full crisis mode. It was critical to share information, listen to each other and work through different perspectives to reach alignment on a path forward.

AFS stakeholders in countries with no cases were less likely to see the need to end participant programs. People at a much higher risk (e.g., older, poorer or immune-compromised people) perceived the pandemic differently than younger, healthier or more affluent people. In addition, people react differently in a crisis. Some find it hard to see it coming, some latch on to unproven theories to help them keep fear at bay, others have difficulty dealing with uncertainty. Some just panic, while others minimize its severity or treat it very lightly. Fortunately, many remain calm, steady and realistic about its potential impact. Recognizing the differing experiences, needs, perspectives, and responses among your team members and stakeholders should be the baseline for all your communications. It took intense communication and listening to come to an agreement that a pandemic was coming and that AFS needed to act globally.

AFS had to address the on-the-ground situation and government response in each country. This included local resource issues, such as access to health care and personal situations, such as needing to protect elderly parents or grandparents.

For AFS, two weeks of challenging discussions began in late February 2020. In hindsight, we could have appreciated these vastly diverse views more quickly, but none of us had ever experienced a crisis of this nature—a rolling, fast-moving pandemic with wildly different government responses.

Leaders must listen to all the different voices, perspectives and experiences to be able to move forward with the most effective plan. No one will have all the answers and things are rarely black and white. This can add to the challenge of managing a crisis but embracing and addressing differences effectively will enhance your response and ensure alignment with your plans.

Use All the Tools You Have

To be effective in crisis management in the digital age means being able to use social media strategically. There is no crisis management today without a full understanding of how to use new media to listen to conversations around your brand in real time and understand what you do and don't need to respond to. —**Chris Syme, author of Listen, Engage, Respond**

In this era, technology is both friend and foe. It allows for effective communication visually, verbally, in writing and, at least virtually, face-to-face. But juggling the different platforms and using them for the right kinds of communications is challenging. We learned quickly that we needed new ways to ensure that communications kept flowing as effectively from the ground up as they did from the top down. We also found that communication must be rapid, accurate (to the best of our knowledge) and ongoing.

Technology was our ally. With tens of thousands of stakeholders in 70 countries, getting the right people the right information every day was daunting. We spent countless hours on wave calls and daily videoconferences, while developing supporting documents for stakeholders and sharing them via channels like Workplace, email and text.

Videoconferencing was the real savior as we could see each other and conduct orderly meetings where people took turns talking and listening. It permitted rapid alignment and changes of direction. This would not have been possible on group telephone calls, which only a few years back would have been all we had.

About five days into the full-scale repatriation effort, I began calling each team member toward the end of every day. I asked them all three questions: how are you doing, do you know what you should be working on, and do you have the support you need? Looking back, I believe this was the single most important action I took as team leader during that hectic phase. We were communicating 17 hours a day but connecting with team members one on one, even if briefly, was invaluable.

While all this helped AFS coordinate all of the other crisis teams and leaders, we also had to ensure communication with the broader AFS community and external audiences was aligned and effective. Each AFS office had to communicate constantly with its staff, volunteers, families, and participants and to those making the wave calls.

We coordinated with outside advisors, such as public relations professionals, to ensure all our messaging was similarly managed across all media, and that it was all monitored by our communications team. Our communications team leader was remarkable in coordinating this vast effort. This high level of messaging was one of the most extraordinary successes.

Key Takeaways

- value diversity and promote diverse views and challenging assumptions

- use every possible tool to communicate in the most effective way

- coordinate consistent messaging across all media

3. Set the Tone for Superior Teamwork

[T]he highest levels of influence are reached when generosity and trustworthiness surround your behavior. —**Dale Carnegie, American writer and lecturer**

In a crisis of the magnitude of Covid-19, crisis teams all over the world in all types of businesses undoubtedly added lots of new members. It isn't always possible to build trust immediately, but leaders can set the tone by modeling key behaviors. If the core team already has a high degree of trust from working together over time, as at AFS, maintaining that tone is easier as the team expands and the crisis evolves.

As the crisis unfolded, our team was making dozens if not hundreds of decisions every hour, trying to solve seemingly intractable problems. I was in regular contact with AFS's president. I knew he was stretched to the limit focusing on other aspects of the crisis and that I needed to protect his time. I remember thinking how fortunate I was to have a boss who trusted me to make these decisions. I felt the same way about my team. That made all the difference.

Nothing eats away at a team like internal conflict. Every leader must keep a sharp eye out for conflicts during a crisis because they can spring up in unexpected ways. You may think you don't have time to address them, but in reality, you can't afford not to take the time.

Collaborate

Don't tell people how to do things; tell them what to do and let them surprise you with their results. —**George S. Patton, Jr., World War II Army general**

Team cohesion can make or break a crisis response, because teams have to work together and rely on each other. Effective leaders roll up their sleeves and jump in as team players, delegating where possible to create a collaborative atmosphere.

At AFS, we had no choice but to collaborate. The sheer size of the communications and logistical challenges was beyond the scope of any one team. The international crisis team coordinated with all the AFS member crisis teams around the world. But collaboration on our own team was most effective when we let each other do what we did best and allowed each other to lead effectively in our own areas of responsibility.

That kind of collaboration can only work when everyone has access to all necessary information, with transparency when possible. The only way AFS could make this happen was, unfortunately, by having a lot of meetings. We kept them short, we focused on making decisions or putting smaller teams together to evaluate options when we couldn't decide. We also focused on agility, flexibility and information sharing.

Foster Transparency

The single most important ingredient in the recipe for success is transparency because transparency builds trust. —**Denise Morrison, CEO Campbell Soup Company**

Panic breeds in a vacuum. Effective leaders reach out often and address issues and concerns openly. They acknowledge fear, frustration or difficulty. This keeps communication pathways open and helps everyone move from initial confusion to a clearer sense of the actions that need to be taken.

Transparency means consistently providing the information people need when they need it to understand what is going on, not just what you want them to know. Transparent communication includes reliable follow-up.

When information is unavailable, uncertain, or changing rapidly, effective leaders assure everyone that decisions are based on the best information available. If they don't have answers, they let people know when they expect to have them or when they will report back. This kind of transparency helps people remain calm and on track, even when no resolution is in sight.

Key Takeaways:

- convey trust in your team

- address conflicts immediately and directly, especially those on your team

- share the information team members need. When information is unavailable or changing, let them know when you will report back

4. Provide Support

I've learned that people will forget what you said, people will forget what you did, but people will never forget how you made them feel.
—Maya Angelou, American poet, author

Leaders support their team by taking the time to find out how each person can contribute best. They help team members grow and give them opportunities to be leaders themselves. At AFS, supporting each other on the team took many forms.

In daily calls with my team in the first week, I could see fatigue setting in. Within a week, two members of our team were sick with Covid-19. I was concerned we would overextend ourselves and get sick or make mistakes.

After repeatedly asking my team members to take a day off and let their backups take over, I realized that no one would take a day off unless I did. So, my backup team leader and I conspired to make it at least appear that each of us was taking a day off. He went off-line for a day and then I did. Immediately, people started coordinating days off. That was critical because, as we all now know, Covid-19 has been an ultra-marathon of a crisis.

Team leaders have to take care of themselves, and they have to make sure team members take care of themselves. Rest and a clear head are more important in a crisis than at any other time. Ensuring that people take a break, checking in regularly and encouraging your team to do its best are small ways you can keep everyone functioning at the highest level.

It is just as important to show support by being flexible. Many of us had children now home full-time or sick family members. Allowing team members to make work adjustments when their own crises hit can make a tremendous difference. Providing the support your team needs can move your team from functioning at peak level to struggling to move forward.

Key Takeaways

- build trust by collaborating and being supportive

- create opportunities for team members to grow and take on leadership roles

- encourage and support self-care

5. Practice Active Listening

If you aren't listening, you aren't learning. —**Lyndon Johnson (former U.S. President)**

Active listening is a skill often used in conflict resolution. It requires full concentration to pay close attention, show you are listening, defer judgment, respond appropriately and provide feedback. Active listening builds strong relationships by establishing rapport and trust. It creates strong teams that are aligned and informed.

Crisis team members responsible for participant support expressed a serious concern almost immediately: how to support students returning home early as well as those who had to shelter in place until they could get home. We knew those who had to shelter in place would strain host families, especially since most schools closed within days of AFS's decision. Host families themselves were trying to stay safe. For this reason, AFS immediately put a team together to support all support staff more robustly with daily and weekly videoconference calls. These staff were responsible for supporting participants and host families, so it was critical they had all the resources and information they needed.

Regular two-way communication among all support staff around the world about their needs and concerns came back to the core crisis team at AFS International. We developed new support approaches, such as enhanced toolkits to work with and support different stakeholder groups, FAQs to answer common stakeholder questions (participants, host families, sending parents, volunteers) and targeted training.

Key Takeaways

- empower your team with nonjudgmental, active listening

- ensure you are hearing from everyone you need to

- adjust or amplify your response to meet needs as they arise

6. Act Decisively

Indecision may or may not be my problem. —**Jimmy Buffet, American singer-songwriter**

Making decisions can be a challenge for all of us. But in a crisis like Covid-19 that evolved with a speed and magnitude that seemed unreal at times, decision-making can be unnerving. The decision-making process should be straightforward, but following it in a pandemic or other extreme crisis is not always easy. The steps are:

1. Define the issue.

2. Evaluate the issue.

3. Evaluate options.

4. Consider the consequences.

5. Make a decision.

During repatriation, each participant's journey was a complex challenge for AFS staff and volunteers. It could take dozens of hours to secure travel for one participant; in some cases, it was impossible. At the same time, each participant's trip home was unlike anything he or she had experienced or expected. One AFS student's complex trip out of China was chronicled by *The New York Times* in this article:

https://www.nytimes.com/2020/02/03/us/coronavirus-american-student-china.html

Some participants had to fly south to fly north and then back south to reach a gateway departure city. One extreme example was two participants who had to fly from Haikou (in very southern China, close to Hong Kong), to Beijing (northern China, 2,500 km away from Hong Kong), and then fly back south to Hong Kong, on to London, then to Roma/Milan. Their trip home took more than 40 hours. At other times, students arrived at the departure airport only to find their flight cancelled.

Our team and all the AFS crisis teams were deeply inspired by the courage and positive attitude of all those participants. As the crisis team and I saw photos of them masked and ready for takeoff in different cities or landing in their home countries, it kept our spirits up and motivated us all to keep going. We didn't know how the pandemic would play out, but we knew the students were safest with their own families, and we were committed to making that happen if it could be done safely and within government requirements.

Four Guatemalan participants returning home after sheltering in place.

As this effort went into overdrive, the rapid-fire decision-making was exhausting. The crisis team and I had to prioritize which countries to evacuate first, evaluate the safety of any planned travel, develop new policies and procedures, ensure all the right people had all the right information, and finalize dozens of documents daily. I recall falling into bed every night totally drained, as texts came in all night long from around the world. At the international level, decisions were on global policies, communications and support (both of our offices and our participants). Although it didn't seem like it at the time, decision-making at the international level (essentially the headquarters of AFS International) was a small fraction of all the decisions being made by the AFS community around the world. Being able to make decisions quickly at all levels was essential.

The crisis team and I tried in every situation to evaluate issues, options and consequences as a team, using the information we had. Often, we didn't have enough time to discuss these in the larger group. We were constantly throwing issues to subgroups to consider and make a recommendation at the next meeting, which sometimes immediately followed the meeting we were in. This strengthened our teamwork, improved our decision-making, and most important, kept the overall effort on track.

It became clear that leading was more about modeling the right behaviors and enabling others to do their jobs, not controlling outcomes. The most successful crisis leaders during Covid-19 were those who were quick to ask for support wherever they could get it. We had support in abundance in AFS. Everyone stepped up, every day. It was an inspiring response to a terrible situation. Developing this decision-making skill can be done in advance with crisis management tabletop exercises, but nothing beats what can be learned about yourself and your team by going through a major crisis together.

Key Takeaways

- be disciplined about how you make decisions

- empower your team to make decisions whenever appropriate

- seek support wherever you can find it

LEADING IN CRISIS:

CHAPTER 13: How Effective Leaders Stay Inspired

A s a crisis leader, you may well find you are stretched to the limit; there aren't enough hours in the day to address all the problems you're facing, you're up at night worrying, you're constantly "on," planning, rethinking, making decisions. How can you nurture yourself so that you can be your best every day?

1. Align Your Actions With Your Values and Mission

It's not hard to make decisions when you know what your values are. —Roy Disney, long-time senior executive for the Walt Disney Co.

Decision-making is easier when you base decisions on your values. It is equally important to align your actions with your organization's mission and values. Stakeholders are more likely to understand and accept the difficult decisions that must be made if they are grounded in the ethos, mission and values of the organization.

AFS's mission is to provide "intercultural learning opportunities to help people develop the knowledge, skills and understanding needed to create a more just and peaceful world." The AFS mission and values, along with its commitment to keeping participants safe (a core value of AFS), are on a single page on AFS's website.

https://afs.org/about-afs/#afs-nav-mission-values

AFS's risk management program has been built in the past 30 years on the core value of keeping participants safe. It is a guiding principle of the AFS crisis management approach. But the team knew that to manage this crisis properly, AFS crisis teams had to align with the organization's other core values— dignity, respect for differences, harmony, sensitivity and tolerance. That meant doing our best to model these behaviors on the team as well as in AFS's decisions and communications.

One issue that came up was that some people outside China began to blame Asians for the spread of the virus, at times harassing people on the street who they thought looked Chinese. As soon as we heard this, we began talking with our other AFS offices. We developed materials to help ensure that our Asian participants were fully supported.

We knew we had to keep an eye on this to keep our participants safe. We asked that any evidence of harassment or abuse be reported to us immediately. Staff in each host country kept these communication and support channels open at all times. Fortunately, AFS participants experienced few and relatively minor incidents.

Part of the AFS mission is to carry out these exchange programs, so closing them down was, without question, AFS's last resort. However, because participant safety is a core value, once it became clear we were dealing with a pandemic of extreme uncertainty, we had no choice.

Explaining the decision to the entire AFS community and the reason for it was challenging. The 12 criteria released in late February (see chapter 2) helped immensely, as did the team evaluation of every return trip through the lens of participant safety. Another challenge was that when we began repatriation, most of the rest of the world was experiencing very few cases. That meant parents, depending on where they lived, had vastly different views. Some sending parents did not want their children home because the virus was spreading there; some host families didn't want the children to leave because the virus had not yet arrived there and they didn't see the need.

Participants under age 18 are AFS's most vulnerable stakeholders, but the safety of all our stakeholders is critical. We considered safety and wellbeing in every decision. For example, at times it was not possible to move participants because the travel that staff, volunteers or host families would have had to undertake to get participants to the airport was unsafe or restricted. In those cases, the student sheltered with the host family.

While situations and plans change moment by moment in a crisis, leaders must remain steadfast. Grounding decision-making in your own values and those of your organization helps you stay the course. Keeping a steady hand and maintaining calm are essential to keep the team on track. I recall the president of AFS at one meeting reflecting, "We need to ask ourselves, what would the (ambulance) drivers (who founded AFS) do?" It was an elegant reminder to stay grounded in our mission and values.

We did have to make course corrections, but I never doubted our decision-making, because it was aligned with AFS's and my own values. This wasn't something I thought about during the crisis, but looking back, I see how much easier it made my work. It was not surprising to me that my own values aligned so closely with AFS's. Not only had I worked there for decades, but I had also been an AFS student to Paraguay in high school.

Key Takeaways

- be authentic

- maintain integrity by aligning your decisions with your values

- ground everything you do in your organization's mission and values

2. Adopt an Attitude that Inspires

Act with Humility

Humility is not thinking less of yourself; it's thinking of yourself less.—C. S. Lewis, British writer, lay theologian

Humility, or a modest view of one's importance is always valuable, but is essential in a crisis. When leaders model humility, acknowledging they don't have all the answers, they invite the creative ideas of the organization's staff, volunteers, consultants and advisors. A team that feels safe to express differing views, disagree and debate to find solutions together is a high-functioning team. Humility underpins effective leadership in a crisis. Its absence can shut down communications and stifle problem solving.

Convey Quiet Confidence

A good leader inspires people to have confidence in the leader; a great leader inspires people to have confidence in themselves.— **Eleanor Roosevelt, former First Lady of the United States.**

Conveying confidence means believing in yourself to the point that you know that success is the only option. Your team will sense this and respond. This is not false bravado; it is faith in yourself and your team. If you interact with others with confidence and respect, you model a core behavior others will follow. Confidence is a two-way street. Crisis leaders who give their team credit for work well-done and encourage the team to think creatively to solve problems pave the way for successful crisis management.

Key Takeaways

- create a safe environment for people to express different views

- lead your team with confidence and respect

- invite your team to think creatively and give credit for work well done

3. Focus on the Big Picture

From the inside looking out, you can never see how it looks from the outside looking in. —**Big Sean, American rapper, singer**

It's easy to get distracted and mired in the details of a crisis. Effective leaders value the details but maintain a big picture perspective. They focus on business continuity and minimizing risk and loss. They look beyond the immediate priorities and adjust objectives and goals as circumstances shift. Leaders also look to similar organizations and outside experts to ensure they are thinking through the broader impact of their decisions.

Throughout the crisis, AFS reached out to other high school exchange organizations, governments, travel advisors and health specialists, public relations firms and other experts to ensure we were seeing the broader picture and getting the best advice. We relied on experts affiliated with AFS throughout the world to evaluate risk, how and when we might resume programs, and importantly, what AFS needed to do to survive financially.

Finances were critical, as they were for virtually every business on the planet. The legal team worked with the finance team to renegotiate every contract we could. We tapped into government support in countries where it was available. We restructured operations at AFS International and around the world. As a last resort, sadly, we had to let go a number of staff. This was heartbreaking because these team members had worked incredibly hard and had been totally committed during the crisis.

The only way crisis leaders can focus on the big picture is if everyone else is empowered to manage the details. For AFS, that meant the communications team did all it could to ensure everyone got necessary information. The finance team addressed fiscal challenges, the legal team worked on contracts, support teams focused on participant wellbeing and support staff, and the board of trustees looked at policies and a framework to direct the organization in a financially stable way. Ultimately, the goal remains business continuity and managing the crisis so that it has the least possible negative impact.

Key Takeaways

- focus on business continuity and reducing the impact of the crisis

- consult with peers, experts and others to gather facts and keep perspective

- delegate the details to others so you can focus on the big picture

4. Stay Agile and Flexible

Stay committed to your decisions but stay flexible in your approach.—**Tony Robbins, American motivational speaker**

Effective leaders are agile. They constantly question assumptions and adapt, adjust and change directions as the situation changes.

Because AFS operates all over the world, the organization has had years of experience adapting and changing direction to manage crises. AFS was created in crisis. It started as a volunteer ambulance corps that took the wounded of all nations off battlefields and rescued survivors from the Bergen-Belsen concentration camp before it adopted its mission of peace through understanding. Since then, AFS has had more than half a million participants, primarily on year-long high school exchanges.

As Covid-19 evolved, it became clear that AFS needed to adapt rapidly, to shift and even change direction as it tried to bring participants home and support stakeholders. We quickly realized we could not bring every participant home at the same time. We developed a three-phased approach, first evacuating countries with health care systems most at risk, then countries with smaller staff and support structures, and finally countries where Covid-19 was spreading rapidly and taxing local infrastructure and hospitals.

However, global travel was in turmoil with countries closing borders daily, others blocking through travel, and airlines canceling flights at the last minute. Our three-phased approach quickly shifted to an evolving series of evacuations when and where possible, driven by external events.

We kept a daily tally of participants still on program; we evaluated chartering our own planes and pushed governments for travel support for their citizens. So many participants had unique travel challenges that we had to consider every option and be ready to change plans. For example, if we couldn't arrange travel because countries were not allowing through travel for people from the host country, we looked to governments to help with repatriation.

In addition to the logistical issues, we had deep concerns about the stress on host families with participants who couldn't get home and might be quarantined with them for weeks. We added resources to build up our support staff, bringing in some of our most experienced former staff to help AFS International's office staff responsible for support.

We launched weekly support staff videoconference calls, rolled out multiple toolkits, and within two weeks launched online learning modules to support participants who traveled and those who could not yet travel.

Key Takeaways

- keep questioning your assumptions

- be ready to add or move team members to different roles

- change directions or approaches whenever that makes sense

5. Stay Visible and Available

In a crisis, don't hide behind anything or anybody. They're going to find you anyway. –**Bear Bryant, former Alabama football coach**

Staying present, being visible and being available at all times—especially to core team members—is critical. Team members need to feel supported. There are many ways to stay visible. It is critical for a leader to be seen leading, responding to questions, listening to advice, keeping the overall effort on track and keeping the team engaged, active and optimistic.

Staying visible as a team leader — and for team members leading other teams — became staying online in videoconferences. We held hundreds of videoconference calls for different constituencies. While this made it easier to stay visible, it became increasingly difficult to stay available. I found I was spending all my time on calls and conferences.

I made myself available in my daily calls with each team member. In these one-on-one conversations, team members felt safe to share things that would not come up in a team meeting. It was a chance to say whatever was on our minds, share the stress, celebrate successes and organize for the next day. That helped strengthen the team, deepen trusts and promote honest, meaningful communication.

Silly Hat Celebration after getting more than 4,000 participants home in two weeks.

Published courtesy of AFS Intercultural Programs and its staff.

Creativity and adaptability are central to balancing time demands and taking care of yourself (see below), so you can show up ready and refreshed every morning.

Key Takeaways

- manage your time so you can be available

- use whatever tools are available to you to lead, listen and respond

- be creative and adaptable in caring for yourself and your team

6. Be Kind

Be kind whenever possible. It is always possible.—Dalai Lama, spiritual leader of Tibet

Effective leaders stay positive and are respectful, patient and kind. Leaders motivated by kindness build trust and confidence. This inspires team members to do their best, especially in stressful times when demands are high.

Crises have a way of bringing everyone's feelings to the surface. Effective leaders manage not only their own emotions but also those of their staff, customers and other stakeholders through effective communication. One simple but crucial component of kindness in a crisis is acknowledging that everyone is, to differing degrees, operating outside his or her comfort zones as each faces significant to extreme uncertainty.

Kindness is critical in extreme crises, because mistakes happen when people are tired, hungry, over-stressed, anxious or fearful. It's hard to imagine anyone during the Covid-19 pandemic who didn't face some or all of these feelings. Many of the challenges the pandemic brought hit close to home. Food supplies disappeared from store shelves. Schools closed. People had to self-quarantine and far too many lost their jobs.

Every adult on the planet was forced to become a crisis manager, though many didn't realize it. Most of us had a particularly difficult time adjusting to months of quarantine with the added responsibilities that brought—caring for children or sick relatives, financial strain, and lack of customary social interaction. Being as supportive as possible is critical in leading through this type of crisis.

Kindness is offering encouragement and emotional support where possible. Simple acts go a long way. For example, if a team member had to miss a meeting to manage a personal issue, I would bring them up to speed when they were available. We regularly traded off chairing meetings and taking the lead on issues.

My backup team leader has 20 years' experience managing crises and was as capable as I at dealing with day-to-day issues, so early on we started rotating responsibilities. This sent a signal to other team members to share work with their backups and modeled the teamwork we wanted and needed.

It's hard to comprehend the challenges all the front-line workers, epidemiologists, grocery store workers, pharmacists, government officials and so many others faced. But responding with kindness is always right, always helpful, and in times of crises, essential to a sustained response.

Key Takeaways

- Encourage and support your team at all times

- Acknowledge the challenges and feelings people are experiencing

- Go the extra mile to always be kind, including to yourself

7. Take Care of Yourself and Your Team

If you want others to be happy, practice compassion. If you want to be happy, practice compassion. —**Dalai Lama**

Leaders who practice self-compassion and have self-care habits, like exercise, meditation, getting enough sleep and eating well have a head start. One of the unique issues of Covid-19 is that it has lasted so long and included extended time sheltering in place, which made access to typical routines difficult or impossible. This made self-care all the more critical. Even those with fixed, stable routines were challenged to maintain them while working long days. In a crisis that goes on for weeks or months, it's easy to forget your own self-care *and* ensure everyone on your team stays rested and focused.

While I maintained my meditation practice and went outside with my sons for 20 minutes every day to throw a football around, I knew I wasn't doing enough. I felt I simply couldn't keep up, which added to the overall stress. For leaders, acknowledging and supporting self-compassion and modeling it where possible becomes most important. Here are a few tips:

- Take care of yourself—Do your best to eat healthy, exercise and get sleep.

- Connect with others—Share your concerns and how you are feeling with a friend or family member. Maintain healthy relationships, even if via video calls.

- Take breaks—Make time to unwind and remind yourself that strong feelings will fade. Take deep-breathing breaks. Try to do activities you usually enjoy.

- Stay informed—When you think you are missing information, you may feel more anxious. Stay up on the information you need to manage your situation.

- Avoid too much exposure to news—Take breaks from the news. Balance news with enjoyable activities, as the news tends to highlight many of the stressors.

- Seek help when needed—leaders need support, too, and taking a break to talk with someone about how you're feeling can make all the difference.

It's hard to imagine that anyone in the Covid-19 pandemic did not experience stress and feel that he or she could have done a better job at self-care. In retrospect, we can identify these missing elements, note them without judgment and plan ways to better incorporate them.

Key Takeaways

- model self-compassion by taking care of yourself in visible ways

- don't be too hard on yourself in a crisis; focus on doing the best you can

- support your healthy relationships by staying connected.

8. Look for Opportunities and Stay Optimistic

A time of crisis is not just a time of anxiety and worry. It gives a chance, an opportunity, to choose well or to choose badly.— **Desmond Tutu, South African Anglican Archbishop and Nobel Peace Prize winner**

As this book is written, the pandemic crisis continues around the world and continues to be a crisis for AFS. It is tragic and endlessly challenging. But it is important for leaders to stay positive and to continue to look for opportunities.

At AFS, as soon as we announced the program closure, we launched a small group to adapt AFS's online intercultural learning program—the Global Competence Certificate or

GCC—for participants returning early or sheltering in place. The group rolled out the program in a little over a week. It was a remarkable effort and a great example of how it's possible to find opportunities in dire situations. While this supported participants, it also became a new AFS offering that enhances our impact and reach in the long term.

We also realized it might be some time before travel would resume normally, so the GCC team initiated three new online intercultural learning products for students to gain intercultural learning insights without traveling. AFS shifted with the crisis to survive, and we found creative ways to grow and change, to adapt to the new reality.

We used key stakeholder groups as sounding boards for some big picture decisions the board of trustees would need to make to keep the organization well-positioned for the future as repatriation continued. Opportunities to partner with similar, like-minded organizations emerged.

We also developed a traffic light system to evaluate and manage risks to determine where we could re-open safely. In September 2020, AFS exchange programs restarted in more than 20 countries. AFS continues to closely monitor conditions for programs on a country-by-country basis to help ensure that every AFSer stays safe while on the program.

We tend to want to continue operating as we have because it is comfortable and feels safe. But it is often in examining fears, losses and uncertainty that leaders can find opportunities. Leaders help people manage these emotions and redirect their energy to possibilities and opportunities, helping everyone stay optimistic.

This is how the crisis team and I discovered new ways of doing business, including extending our online offerings to young people who were not even going on an AFS program.

Key Takeaways

- stay upbeat with your team, regardless of the news

- manage uncertainty and fear by looking for the opportunities

- focus on the future as you manage the current crisis

This list of essential leadership behaviors is far longer than most crisis managers might have thought important before Covid-19, but they were the elements that changed everything in the way we managed the crisis at AFS.

PART FOUR. LEARNING FROM THE EXPERIENCE

LEADING IN CRISIS:

CHAPTER 14: How to Conduct a Post-crisis Evaluation

One of the biggest opportunities of a crisis is what you can learn from it. Unfortunately, it can be difficult to get a post-crisis evaluation done immediately after a crisis, as people strive to get life and work back to some level of normalcy. They're tired and they want a break from the crisis. To be effective, however, the evaluation should be done when the experience is fresh in everyone's minds.

For AFS, program closure and repatriation were a tremendous crisis, but when that was achieved, the global pandemic was far from over. AFS simply shifted to address the next phase: business continuity and planning for the future in a rapidly changing world. It was not easy to gain support to evaluate the first part of an ongoing crisis, but we knew it was critical to do before everyone refocused on the new challenges.

Our experience of the global pandemic has been more of a series of crises, much like the Shackleton Expedition; it has gone on and on and changed from one crisis to another with different critical objectives.

High-performing teams have long known that an immediate post-crisis review reveals opportunities to change approaches to be more effective. Organizations can analyze policies, decisions and actions to see what worked well, what could be improved and what should be abandoned as no longer useful. A review may also reveal the need for new policies and procedures. it often prompts changes to the organization's crisis plan itself.

To be effective, everyone participating must feel safe to offer insights, questions and criticism without fear of retribution. This means, for example, that findings should NOT be part of performance appraisals. People must look honestly at their own roles to identify areas they can improve.

The idea is to focus on results and identify actions the organization can take to improve its approach to crises. It may be possible to incorporate what's been learned into other areas of the business where innovative actions were especially successful.

Despite AFS's long experience with crises, we had to be especially agile to manage the constantly changing landscape of Covid-19. This compelled us to try new things constantly. It was clear early on that many innovations worked so well they could be adapted and used in other situations. It was equally clear that there was room for improvement. This is why a post-crisis evaluation is always important. We knew, for example, that the crisis plan itself had to be re-written to better address global crises as large as pandemics. For our crisis planning, Covid-19 changed everything.

The challenge in conducting a post-crisis evaluation for the program closure and repatriation portions of the crisis was to reach all the stakeholders for input and feedback. These included the AFS International crisis team, all the crisis teams and staff in AFS member offices, volunteers, participants, host parents and sending parents.

How do you conduct a post-crisis evaluation? The process is usually fairly simple, though it can be hard to get people to give it the attention it deserves, especially in an ongoing crisis. At AFS, we sent a detailed survey to each AFS member organization. About 80 percent responded. See below for a sample post-crisis checklist.

Once you have leadership support, you are ready to conduct a post-crisis evaluation. You can customize as much as you want, but be sure to cover the basics:

- Did we have a crisis plan?

- Did we follow the plan?

- Did we improvise and if so, why?

- Did our approach change as the situation evolved. If so, why?

- What did others in the industry do, and how do we compare our response to those other organizations?

- What are the key takeaways and lessons learned?

- What can we do now to be better prepared for the next crisis?

- Does what we learned from this experience require modifications to our crisis plan?

- Is there anything we tried that we want to incorporate into our ongoing business?

People must honestly assess themselves and their team's performance at all levels for the post-crisis evaluation to be effective. The goal is constructive analysis and, where appropriate, criticism that results in actionable next steps. It's good to remember that often the most valuable lessons in life come from the most challenging and intense experiences.

The most significant learning for AFS was the overwhelming complexity of the communications challenges facing a large international not-for-profit with a decentralized network of independent yet interdependent entities.

In addition to getting feedback from each of the AFS member organizations, we also surveyed our own crisis team members on the international staff and our customers—the participants. The survey showed participants were unhappy that AFS cut the program short, but the vast majority understood the decision was based on their safety and wellbeing, showing that grounding our decisions in our values helped manage expectations. The Special Edition GCC online program was critical in connecting participants to each other and AFS during a challenging time so they could process their experience. This significantly enhanced their views about AFS support during the crisis.

Some of the key findings for AFS were:

1. Daily wave calls to every one of the AFS offices to learn their concerns, issues and needed support were extremely valuable.

2. Supporting AFS participants, whether they were returning early or sheltering in place, with the adapted online learning program was very important.

3. All stakeholders viewed communications extremely positively, but it was equally clear that it was impossible to communicate precisely the right information to the right people at the right time every step of the way. This was primarily because of the constantly changing environment and the diverse array of AFS stakeholders in more than 60 countries.

4. Technology, especially videoconferencing, was a lifesaver, both for communications and for proper execution of the dramatic and complex repatriation of so many young people.

5. All our crisis plans needed to be reviewed and revised to address global crises like pandemics and changes in communications methods since our last review.

6. It is critical to have enough crisis team members with training or solid experience so there is always an awareness of the plan, of each person's unique role, and of the big picture.

My crisis team and I found many things we needed to change immediately, including our entire repatriation travel plan. We also found that we were providing too much information to some stakeholder groups and too little to others. Finding the right balance and treating each stakeholder group separately and thoughtfully is critical and we keep adjusting to try to achieve this.

Key Takeaways

- post-crisis evaluations are valuable opportunities for an organization to learn, grow and prevent or minimize the next crisis

- everyone involved has to feel safe to be honest about what worked, what didn't, and what can be improved

- Covid-19 created extreme communications challenges and has required constant adjustment of approaches and strategies

Every organization should have a crisis plan to frame its crisis response. Team members should know their roles and receive training in advance. One of the best ways to ensure your crisis plan is exactly right for your organization is to do an honest, thorough post-crisis evaluation and then improve all areas you identify in that review.

Sample Post-crisis Evaluation Checklist

Each stakeholder group should have its own questionnaire.

Team functions: team leader, internal communications, external communications, documenter, human relations, legal, public relations.

For all answers please rate as **Extremely Well, Well, Fair,** or **Poor.**

Please give a detailed explanation after each answer.

    1. How do you feel that the crisis was managed overall?

:-) ☒ ☒ ☒ ☒ :-(

    2. How successfully did the Crisis Response Team **work together?**

:-) ☒ ☒ ☒ ☒ :-(

    3. How well did the team deal well with **internal** stakeholders and requirements?

:-) ☒ ☒ ☒ ☒ :-(

    4. How well did the team deal well with **external** stakeholders and requirements?

:-) ☒ ☒ ☒ ☒ :-(

5. How prepared was the team to deal well with **the media**?

:-) ☒ ☒ ☒ ☒ :-(

6. Was a consistent, ongoing **crisis report** always available?

Yes ☒ No ☒

7. Is there a **complete crisis file**, noting all actions from beginning to end (documenter)?

Yes ☒ No ☒

8. Was there any point at which the crisis seemed to have changed for better or worse? When did that happen?

9. Were there any areas where you felt that management of the crisis could have been improved?

10. What **procedures** could you implement to improve future crisis management??

CHAPTER 15: Anticipating Crises— Tabletop Exercises

O ne of the best ways to prepare your crisis team is through tabletop exercises that use crisis scenarios to teach team members how to react in crises. What should your tabletop crisis scenario be about? Build it around what you think your team needs to be prepared to face. These scenarios will be strikingly different from organization to organization.

For example, a power blackout could cause a crisis for a business, such as a dairy. Here the focus must be on the repercussions, such as snarled transportation, loss of inventory, disruption of infrastructure, lack of support, and inability to communicate.

Dream up a scenario that features these effects and compels your team to find ways to deal with the challenges. After that, they will not only be able to deal with the risk of blackout, but also with any crisis that presents the same sorts of problems.

Think about the top five crises that could affect your organization. Recall the definition of crisis—what could happen suddenly or unexpectedly that could derail your organization so significantly that your senior managers would have to drop what they're doing to deal with the crisis? What situation could shut your organization down if you were unable to respond well?

A good way to determine this is by using the five "Ws"—who, what, when, where and why. Who could be involved that could trigger a crisis like that? Which of your stakeholders might be most significantly involved? What event, action or inaction could cause a crisis ? What circumstance could create vulnerability?

When might your organization be particularly vulnerable to crisis? Where could a crisis occur. and why is the location significant? Finally, what is the crisis concern that keeps you up at night and why?

Key Takeaways

- use detailed examples of the types of crises that could halt business

- determine the skills and knowledge your team needs to manage a crisis and its repercussions

- create time-sensitive scenarios that replicate the potential crises that keep you up at night

How Training Promotes Preparation

Once you've built your crisis team, give them an opportunity to become familiar with the crisis toolkit and build the team dynamic with a crisis management dry run. The key is to come up with a compelling scenario with significant detail and a challenge the team can grapple with in less than three hours. Don't hesitate to add some humorous elements. That will help lighten the exercise.

Build redundancy by creating double coverage: a front-line team member and a backup. Use the tabletop session to train both sets of teams at the same time. That ensures everyone is prepared. It is always interesting to compare how different teams assess and resolve crisis issues.

To begin, produce the scenario, explain the rules, and set the timer. The first step is for each team member to consult the crisis packet and jump into action. It's not second nature for people to reach for crisis information under such circumstances—part of the value of the exercise is to help team members recognize the need to use their crisis tools. You can decide whether to provide the crisis toolkit or challenge team members to put their hands on their own copies in real time.

Once teams have the basic information, each should work as a group in a separate room. The team will determine the level of crisis it is facing, the roles team members should play, and how to fill those roles. The team leader will use the team leader checklist to work with the group to develop a response plan that includes timelines, decision-making and communications plans.

A major benefit of tabletop training is that it teaches a team to work with a sense of urgency and accountability. The degree to which speed and initiative are critical in crisis response can be surprising for new team members. It's helpful for them to experience just how swiftly and effectively they will need to work together in real time.

An additional benefit of this exercise is that potential crisis team leaders can evaluate who is best at what roles, who handles pressure well and who stays focused on achieving goals. We all have different leadership styles and personal strengths and weaknesses. It is never more important than in a crisis for the team leader to know how best to deploy his or her team and how to support each team member to maintain team cohesion, momentum and optimism.

Each team member will use the team member checklist to help develop five to 10 action steps he or she will be responsible for to further the team response. Your scenario should require some team members to do research (you might provide some research to clarify the specifics of the scenario) and others to cope with unclear or insufficient detail, as is often necessary in a developing crisis.

Require trainees to do their tasks within the deadlines the team sets. In a three-hour exercise, the timeline is short. That helps the team see how their work aids or hinders initial decision-making and how it affects next steps. They can also see how they can apply the experience to a crisis that spans a much longer time.

Typically, a team member will work through several cycles during a tabletop exercise—doing the initial assessment, helping form a response plan, taking on several tasks, following up, taking on more tasks, following up, then helping bring the exercise to resolution. Those who have gone through this experience turn out to be very useful in an actual crisis.

Key Takeaways:

- ensure each team member has a backup

- train the backup team as you train the team

- use the opportunity to evaluate each member's strengths and weaknesses

LEADING IN CRISIS:

CHAPTER 16: Leadership Lessons from Others

F ortunately, we experience world-changing crises fairly rarely, but Covid-19 is one of those crises. We will come out of this storm changed, but we hope stronger. It may take years for global and local economies to rebound fully. Businesses will also change to meet the changing demands of a new world. World politics are likely to change as well.

Maybe most important, we must realize that we are all crisis managers in our own way. Just as we need to use best practices in our businesses to manage crises, we must do the same in our own lives. All of us must constantly reassess our goals and objectives to **evolve with the crisis**. For AFS, the Covid-19 crisis began with the repatriation of young participants and evolved into supporting them online. From there it moved to preserving the global network, finding a way to continue to pursue AFS's core mission through diverse activities and safely restarting exchange programs.

AFS saw the importance of staying true to our values and mission during a crisis when we announced that we were carefully restarting programs just six months after closing and saw reactions like these on social media:

"Wow!! Almost 20 years ago I was in the same place. About to start the very best year of my life. Congrats, AFS, and welcome new AFSers!"

"This is awesome news for the lucky new AFS students!"

"AFS profoundly changes your life for the good; it also helps you to better understand others through empathy. I loved my experience and have never looked back on it with regret but with awe! Thank you AFS for making me a better global citizen!"

What else can we learn from this crisis? Here are some lessons others have learned about leadership during the Covid-19 pandemic:

Attitudes Can Inspire

"I think of it as an act of radical optimism," said Lacy Schutz, Executive Director of the Shaker Museum and Library in New Lebanon, NY, describing the museum's response to the pandemic. "The Shakers were radical optimists— they had great belief in what they did and in their future. We talk about it on the board and at the committee and staff levels. There is an opposite shore. We will get beyond this. We will get to a point where we can be together again."

"I never thought my church was the building. I always knew it was the people," said the Rev. Canon Tanya Wallace, Rector of All Saints' Episcopal Church in South Hadley, MA. "But when we could no longer use the building, I had to find new ways of supporting and nurturing the parish community."

Rev. Wallace moved worship services to Zoom, and, she said, "the community found surprising blessings in seeing each other's faces rather than the backs of their heads."

She found her parish community needed more support and began Compline, or bedtime prayer services, on Zoom. "Now we pray together seven days a week, and the community has both expanded and deepened."

She found creative ways to bring the community together online—a book group, a study of the theology of Broadway musicals, and a knitting group. She mailed palm crosses during Holy Week and, with her daughter Rebecca's help, planted lawn signs at every house proclaiming, "We are never apart—maybe in distance, but never in heart."

Teamwork Makes All the Difference

Dr. Sergio Angulo Castro, MD, PhD, a neurology resident at a New York City hospital, likened the early days of the pandemic to being thrown into a war without weapons or protection.

"While it took us much longer than we would have liked to get it together, a few things made a big difference. The first was people stepping up—and not necessarily people in power, but people in the middle—chief residents, head nurses, and members of the Coronavirus Taskforce, which was formed on the fly.

"The second was teamwork," he said. His department moved to videoconferencing for coordination but also to check frequently on how everyone was faring emotionally and mentally.

Employees hunted for resources to help the team. "A South Korean colleague got doctors at home to ship us about 80 hazmat suits at a time when PPE (personal protective equipment) was impossible to find."

Equally important, he said, "We backed each other up."

Medical residents aren't allowed to take sick days or mental health days and are entitled to only one day of paid parental leave. "The expectation is that you show up to work no matter what. But people really looked out for one another. Some of my colleagues who are unmarried or don't have small children volunteered to take the most dangerous roles. That was an incredible act of teamwork, humanity, and personal sacrifice."

That kind of teamwork made all the difference for Dr. Castro because his wife was eight months pregnant when the pandemic hit. "It was extremely stressful and, quite frankly, terrifying," he admitted. "My colleagues got together and covered me for a week so that I could be there when my wife delivered, and also at home with the baby. They switched shifts with me so that for the first three weeks of the baby's life, I had the least dangerous rotations."

Active Listening Helps Build Trust

Sara Loughlin, mother of two, said it hasn't been easy having to say, "I don't know," to so many of her kids' questions about the future, but she finds if she focuses on the days ahead, her kids trust her to share information as it becomes available.

Loughlin is careful to check in with her children before they make plans to create the structure each needs. "I had to make space for them to feel seen and heard, to understand and validate their thoughts and feelings," she said. One needs intense work projects, the other needs long periods of alone time. "Each has needed more of those things in the pandemic," said Loughlin.

Decisive Leaders Motivate Their Team

"In times like this, we can't be messing around and guessing—leaders need to be clear, direct, swift, and pivot to look at the brutal facts," said Brad Rogers, headmaster of the Gow School in South Wales, NY for students with dyslexia and other language-based learning disabilities. "I reject the concept of social distancing— it's physical distancing. We need to socialize more than ever. I remember saying to my employees, "We will be open. We will have students on campus. We got this. If you are worried or concerned, join me. We have a strategy and a plan."

That strategy, and Rogers' vision and confidence allowed the private school to operate in person in the summer of 2020 and directly into the academic year. Rogers remains on alert. "When it lands here, and it will, we have a quarantine system, contact tracing, all the procedures, we are not going to light our hair on fire," he said.

"If there's one thing I've learned," said Rev. Wallace, "it is that even when we don't know where we are going, the best thing to do always is to stick together and do the next right thing."

Although seminary training does not cover leadership in a time of crisis, Rev. Wallace said, "I have yet to serve a parish that hasn't faced a significant crisis." She was rector of her first parish in downtown Manhattan on 9/11, received a death threat for presiding at a Civil Union in Vermont amidst statewide turmoil over gay marriage. And within four months of her arrival at her current parish, a high school student committed suicide after prolonged bullying, which enfolded the town in a years-long healing process.

Stay True to Values Creates a Path Forward

"When Covid hit, we were firing on all cylinders to meet the needs of the public," said Marybeth Mills, proprietor of the Peekamoose Restaurant in Big Indian, NY. "Community outreach is important to us, so we participated in Project Resilience, an Ulster County, NY initiative to help feed the elderly, and Feed the Frontline (a program to provide meals for first responders and vulnerable community members). "Safety and health were paramount, so making sure the public was safely cared for was essential to us. Don't think we weren't terrified ourselves, but keeping busy and taking it day by day is helping us get through this."

For the All Saints' church community, "While our church is closed, we have become church," Rev. Wallace said. "We have reached beyond the walls we can't inhabit. We have made and donated masks, made and donated meals for the homeless, held outdoor services that included collecting non-perishables for the local food pantry and warm hats and mittens for local college students stuck on a near-deserted campus.

"After the murder of George Floyd, I organized a Black Lives Matter vigil, which led to a weekly online group of support and accountability for folks to lean into the work of acknowledging white supremacy and taking steps to address racism," she said.

Look for Certainty, but Stay Open to Pivot

"With a crisis, frequently comes a tremendous upending force of chaos. Up feels like down. Left appears right. Night is day," said Matthew Doering, Founder and CEO of Global Gateway Advisors, a communications consultancy that works with an array of private and nonprofit organizations on crisis preparedness and response.

Doering helps clients open to learning and look for some certainty while remaining flexible. "For as unpredictable, uncontrollable and unprecedented as any crisis event can seem, there are always learnings and patterns from other cases that inform how we handle what is happening now and prepare for what is next," he said. "Look for ways to bring certainty into uncertain times. Work off a plan—but commit to the principle of 'freedom within the framework.' It's important to be open to adapt, reshape or pivot plans as new information or elements of the situation change."

Schutz and her team at the Shaker Museum pivoted quickly. "Just about when Covid hit, we were quick to say absolutely no to our gala. We knew we were not going to be fine by August and we were not going risk having the gala be a super-spreader event. We pivoted to create an online event when there hadn't been many online galas. We wanted to create intimacy and excitement online."

The museum created a VIP cocktail party for paying donors and honorees, but made the gala itself free and open to anyone who wanted to attend. "People joined in from all over the country—people who had never participated before," Schutz said. "Even though the average donation size was down, the number of donors was up 43 percent over last year."

153

The Big Picture Has its Own Demands

While attending to the challenges and opportunities of the moment, Rev. Wallace said, "I am trying to lead the congregation into an unknown future, in the hope and promise of our faith, which is that not in spite of, but right in the midst of death and loss, we are promised new life. Our parish community has been changed by this time. We have no desire to return to 'normal,' but yearn to incorporate what we have learned as we move into the next manifestation of church. Not going to church. Being church, together."

At the Gow School, Rogers leads by example—wearing a mask and practicing physical distancing to model the behaviors that keep his staff and students healthy. But he found fear of Covid required more attention, action and engagement than the actual disease. "That takes more time than keeping the community physically healthy," he said.

Maintain a Presence

Christopher Lukach, APR, President of AKCG—Public Relations Counselors, found the perception of inadequate response is a risk many mission- and values-driven organizations are facing during the pandemic, especially those entrusted with the care of others, such as long-term health care providers and hospitals. "This has been exacerbated by inadequate communication," he said, "either in substance or frequency."

"The pandemic hit just a few weeks before our annual conference, an important source of revenue for our nonprofit," said Melissa Torres, President and CEO of The Forum on Education Abroad. "Our field was already reeling from the

CDC's advisory singling students out for repatriation before any other travelers."

Torres wanted to stay visible and offer a forum for peers to talk, share strategies and figure out next steps. The Forum staff jumped at the chance to offer the conference virtually, training more than 120 presenters in just six weeks, setting up 97 virtual exhibit booths, and reworking the plenary and networking events. At the same time that staff were working frantically to prepare for the conference, they also created six free Covid-19 response webinars that more than 1,500 people attended.

"This was already an incredibly strong and dedicated team, but the pandemic has demonstrated the importance of trusting the other people in your lifeboat to keep rowing, bailing, and doing whatever it takes to stay afloat."

The Forum's virtual conference was so successful, it has augmented revenue by planning virtual conferences for other education abroad organizations.

Kindness Motivates

Here is how Janice Abraham, CEO of United Educators, described her communications with staff during Covid-19.

"I have learned that communicating with staff is paramount. It is an opportunity to show humility, empathy and care. I post a message on our intranet every evening. Some personal news, some business news, some humor, some frustration and always an attempt to show the staff that I am thinking of them, struggling a bit like they are and that when we stay together, we thrive. I end every message with: Stay safe, wash your hands and be kind. Years ago, an early mentor told me, it doesn't cost much to be a hero. He was right. It takes a heart though."

"While I have always considered myself to be an empathetic parent," Loughlin said, "the pandemic really raised the stakes. I found I had to be more empathetic to myself and my kids, because there was so much more going on. [The kids] need to know they are being seen and cared for before they can perform. Kindness and empathy are the first step. Once people in crisis know they won't be further traumatized by harsh judgments, they will open up and eagerly rejoin the team."

Lukach of AKCG Public Relations Counselors recognizes the importance of creating trust and goodwill among the people an organization serves. The extra effort to offer a compassionate response, even to someone who is angry or afraid, "has a powerful disarming effect," he said. "It is finding ways, in the midst of widespread suffering and uncertainty, to convey our humanity."

Care for Yourself to Care for Others

Robert Brandt, PhD, a clinical psychologist of 45 years, went through a period of despair when Covid-19 hit and quickly realized that to help his clients, "I would have to open my heart more fully."

"I've been a meditator my entire adult life, and I realized the best way was to strengthen and deepen my meditation practice. So, I'm often meditating 1½ hours a day—70 minutes longer than I had been," he said.

That time in meditation has not only renewed his spirit but brought a sense of optimism. "I have begun to consider that as a planet we are perhaps increasing our awareness so we can move beyond the very real limits of our daily perceptions. Opening my heart more fully, which I understand is a privilege

I'm afforded, (so many aren't), gives me a wellspring of positivity and love to draw from and bring to the people I work with to help them find their inner resources to combat very real despair and to adjust, adapt and find resilience."

Finding Opportunities Builds Optimism

Chris Eggemeier, an elementary school teacher at a public school in Amherst MA, feels the overwhelming stress of online schooling as a teacher, and he sees it in his students and in their parents. Yet, he said, "the year has gone well." He has found in the challenge an opportunity "to take a step back into unknowing." This led him to look for ways to "Marie Kondo" the curriculum. In other words, to look at everything and see what sparks joy, what increases student interest and agency, and to thank and let go of anything that no longer serves.

The Wildwood School has 400 students who speak more than 25 home languages. He and his students struggle to understand what is being communicated with the barriers online schooling present.

"Kids are yearning for connection," he said. One way he helped all of them be present was introducing a practice he calls joy-spotting. He asked students to look back on each day for moments of joy and to write about them in a journal. Now, he's looking for ways to apply what he's learned from his students to infuse joy into the school day.

Schutz of the Shaker Museum also found opportunities in the restrictions imposed. "On an institutional level, we found the pandemic reinforcing how critical it is to look at things that seem to be setbacks as opportunities." She said Covid gave them the opportunity to address some of the discomfort they'd already felt about the annual fundraising gala.

"It had a high-ticket price, you had to live in the region, you had to feel comfortable going to that kind of event. So many nonprofit organizations use this fundraising model," she said. Covid "forced us to say, how could we do it differently?"

Restaurateur Mills found she and her chef husband were actually able to grow their business, moving to large heat-at-home meals for carryout and then using their outdoor space during the warmer months not only to meet safety guidelines for distancing but to build a firepit and install a large outdoor screen for movies. Guests kept returning.

"Last night," she recalled, "there were families sitting out on our lawn drinking cocktails under a star-filled sky...the bonfire was blazing, and *The Goonies* was showing on our screen. Kids were roasting marshmallows. It was everything I'd always wanted my restaurant to be."

She is still afraid of the illness, but she said, "I'm newly reinvigorated about the possibilities."

CHAPTER 17: Looking Forward

A s we put the finishing touches on this book, the pandemic continues to rage around the world in second and third waves. We have all struggled to stay healthy and sane; we have all grown weary of wearing masks and physical distancing. People need to work, but as we return to school and work and increase social interaction, Covid-19 surges.

At the same time, health care professionals and science are showing us how much things have changed in 100 years. The mortality rate has dropped dramatically since the pandemic began, with improved understanding and treatment of the virus. Vaccines, unheard of a century ago, are advancing through clinical trials at a breathtaking pace.

During the pandemic, we have seen countries impose severe lockdowns with varying success, while others kept their economies going and seemed to fare reasonably well. In those countries that have been fairly effective in managing the pandemic, leaders have modeled and reinforced behaviors that work. Physical distancing and wearing masks dramatically slow the spread of the virus; those countries and regions where people recognize this and take these simple measures do dramatically better.

Looking forward, facing yet unknown global misfortunes brought on by climate change, forced migration, infectious diseases and a rise of fear and hatred, what can we adopt from Shackleton's powerful example and our own experience? One ingredient is looking out for everyone, especially those who are struggling—the ones who need the mittens or the extra ration of food. Another is finding joy, finding cause for celebration wherever we can. Those celebrations may look different, as the crew discovered, but they had great value even in altered form.

Gratitude is a powerful antidote to hopelessness. Research today shows the benefits of gratitude, but that was something Shackleton knew instinctively. Acts of generosity and meaningful routines protect us from despair and hopelessness *and* benefit others. Shackleton also showed his men the strength of mutual dependence, by assigning everyone to help everyone else, regardless of whether the tasks were in their original job description.

The world is at an inflection point as we battle these second and third and likely fourth waves of the pandemic before an effective vaccine becomes widely available and used. At some point, this pandemic will be over, but other global crises loom. What we do in this time will determine the direction of this arc of history—whether we turn toward creating a better, safer, kinder, more just world for all people, or whether we forgo the discomfort of change and continue with business as usual. We have an opportunity, and that opportunity has enormous consequences for future generations and for the planet itself.

Leadership matters, especially in times like these. It's up to each us to do what we can.

The learnings from others, shared in chapter 16, illustrate how many of us are finding creative ways to be leaders in our own lives, with our families, for our communities, in our organizations, and, by example, in the way we interact with others.

Small actions often have the biggest impact. Here are some that can help:

- model those behaviors that help you stay healthy and grounded

- recognize that we are all in this together

- take care of yourself and support those around you

- be on the lookout for joy and share it where you can

- listen actively to each other

- build trust through compassion and consistency

- be kind, no exceptions

- be present and available whenever possible

- be flexible

- stay optimistic and keep looking for opportunities

- stay humble

- know that everything you do matters.

Finally, keep your values and the big picture in the forefront. It's easy to slip into despair when the news around the world is primarily about division and suffering. But when people come together, we can not only solve immense problems, we can change the world.

If our key takeaway from this incredibly challenging time is to try to forget it and move on to the next "Roaring ⬚20s" once a vaccine is widely used, the next crisis will likely be far worse. It is critical that we take the time now to learn from what we are going through, so that we can manage future crises more effectively.

Climate change in particular looms as the challenge of the 21st century. If we fail to act effectively, we are likely to see mass human migration, greater income disparity and a potentially tragic competition for ever more scarce resources.

It is our hope that these reflections on leadership during times of crisis can help bring us together, not only to manage this pandemic, but to help heal the deep divisions in our communities, countries and across the globe. If we do, we will find the solutions we need not only to address crises arising from climate change, but also to handle all the other crises that lie ahead.

Walk together, talk together, all ye peoples of the earth; then and only then shall ye have peace.—**Ancient Sanskrit proverb and early AFS motto.**

Made in the USA
Middletown, DE
06 September 2021